Affirmative Prayer

.

Becoming Your Own Answered Prayer

"We find that prayer is essential to happiness, for righteous prayer sets the law of the Spirit of life in motion for our good. Prayer is essential to the conscious wellbeing of the soul. Prayer has stimulated countless millions to higher thoughts and better lives. Prayer is its own answer. Before our prayer is framed in words the possibility of its answer already exists."
Dr. Ernest Holmes

CONTENTS

ACKNOWLEDGMENTS

A heartfelt thanks to each and every person I have met and known along my life journey. I am keenly aware that each of you in some way influenced my becoming who I am today, directly impacting my capacity to give, receive, and become more of my True Self.

I have learned trust, compassion, and to see God easily in humanity from those of you who are my friends. Those I believed to betray or hurt me, taught me the power of forgiveness and returning to my Soul where perceived wrong doing was not that at all; but instead a practice of learning to be compassionate.

Those I perceived to break my heart brought me into the power of mending and the discovery of the strength of my heart. Those I believed to take from me in some way, I bow to you for teaching me that nothing can be taken or lost in consciousness. Giving is the currency of Spirit.

You see, my life is blessed, and each day I am dedicated to becoming a more generous giver and gracious receiver, remaining awake to the wonder of this thing called Life.

A special shout out to my prayer partners: Rev. LeeAnn Gibbs, Rev. Teresa Luttrel, and Rhonda Britten who collectively have prayed for and with me for thousands of hours. To my prayer practitioner, Angela C. Montano, who has been in prayer for me for close to ten years.

To my numerous teachers who pointed me toward the Only One: St. Stephen's Episcopal Church, Seattle, faculty of University of Puget Sound Religious Studies Department, Seattle Center for Spiritual Living, Agape Center for International Truth, Holmes Institute, Emerson Theological Seminary, John of God, Dr. Eric Pearl, Jack Elias, Scott Sulak, Kim Lipsman, and the many others.

A big hug to my biological and chosen family.

CHAPTER 1
AFFIRMATIVE PRAYER

"Man will deliver himself from sickness and trouble in exact proportion to his discovery of himself and his true relationship with the Whole."
Dr. Ernest Holmes

A Bit About Me

I remember praying as a little girl before bed, in the mornings and throughout the day as I experienced joy. This may appear to be a normal occurrence in most families, but an odd one in mine, as my family didn't attend church. Yet, within me was a deep yearning for God and I acted from this yearning as a little girl.

At age five I decided I would take myself to church, and I did. I went to the neighborhood Episcopalian church, as it was the closest for my little feet to walk to. Had a Jewish synagogue or a Sikh Temple been down the street, the trajectory of my religious upbringing may have been quite different.

The first day I walked into this majestic old church, I knew it was God's home by its beauty. I almost didn't make it in as the sanctuary doors were easily ten times the size of an average front door and equally heavy. Turning the doorknob and pulling this weighted gate toward me, took an act of faith all of its own. Once open, I tiptoed across the ever-buffed marble floor in front of the sainted stain glass sanctuary so as not to make any noise on a quiet Tuesday afternoon. Aware of the tall ceiling that miniaturized my body even further, I headed down two flights of stairs. My destination was the basement choir room where I would join other five year olds who

1

would be belting out songs showing their love and devotion to God.

My prayer life as a young girl included talking directly to God about things I liked, wanted, found beautiful or questioned. I believed God to be A Big Daddy to everyone, living above the clouds with supersonic ears open to hearing the requests of all. My prayers included singing hymns. I heard someone say a prayer was more powerful if it was sung, and so I sang my prayers, at times, when I believed my prayers were extra important.

I would have my first mystical experience at age five. It was a sunny spring Seattle day and my dad and I planted a radish garden in the backyard. We built up a raised bed using bricks from a nearby home which had been remodeled. We stacked them and filled in the box with planting soil. We prepared the soil with chicken poop, which as a small kid I thought was disgusting and I demonstrated this by plugging my nose with one hand while digging with the other. Once planted, this garden was mine to tend. I pulled weeds, watered, measured growth and loved it. To me, tending wasn't complete without prayer. One day on my knees, singing my prayer followed by the hymn *All Things Bright and Beautiful*, for emphasis, I had a revelation. My body began to quiver, I felt the love of God surrounding me, touching my skin, and I wept from feeling this Invisible Spirit of Divine Love. I promised at that moment I would grow up, become a minister, and serve God.

My attraction to Affirmative Prayer is several fold. I learned this prayer technology twenty plus years ago when I was 28 years old and thought I knew a lot and what I thought I knew didn't satisfy my unquenchable yearning to know God. My prayer life had become stale. Heck, my whole life had become routine and overwhelming. My idea of God as external made connecting with "Him" impossible and my concept of God was contracting by the day.

The practice of Affirmative Prayer began quenching my yearning, shifting my experience of God from an outer experience to an inner one, and bringing me back into the energy field of God/Love I experienced as a young girl in front of her garden. As my practice with this prayer technology deepened, I came to realize Affirmative Prayer as a practice of embodying qualities of God in order to make Heaven visible on earth through me.

History of Affirmative Prayer

Dr. Ernest Holmes, founder of Science of Mind, made Affirmative Prayer popular, although it already existed in various forms and was being taught through the rising American and English spiritual movement. Dr. Holmes says in his book <u>Living the Science of Mind</u>:

"Whatever the difference of opinion among these earlier teachers may have been, they all seem unanimous in emphasizing mental and spiritual causation and the thought that the material universe possesses no independent life and intelligence. Of course, this was before the day of the new physics. They all taught that spiritual mind healing of the physical body is the result of touching the springs of life the soul of the patient." Dr. Ernest Holmes

Dr. Holmes was known as a great assimilator, taking information from a variety of sources and compiling it for useful application. During Holmes' lifetime (1887-1960), the United States was becoming a welcoming place for Eastern religions and philosophies, yoga, spiritual inquiry and metaphysics. Affirmative Prayer, then, became a natural sequencing of demonstrable spiritual practices.

Affirmative Prayer is also referred to as Spiritual Mind Treatment or "treatment." According to the medical community, upward of 80 percent of illness originates in the unconscious or subjective mind or Mind/Emotion realm directly influencing the physical body. Entering into the consciousness, of the Spiritual Realm of one's being, then, can become the answer for healing much psychological and physical illness. As a doctor would prescribe a medication to "treat" a condition, the metaphysician would prescribe a new way of thinking to "treat" the conditioned thought that brings about disease.

Treatment, though, would be applied not only as a curative solution, but also for fulfilling the dream's of in one's life in such areas as success, joy, relationships, and faith.

The words Affirmative Prayer indicate praying from the affirmative alignment with Spiritual Truth. The power of living from an affirming mentality continues today to be scientifically validated as primary factors in success, happiness, lasting relationships, and health.

Holmes credits several individuals to contributing to his formulation of Affirmative Prayer. I have read, studied, applied and respected the work of

3

each pioneering metaphysician, so I will introduce them to you and share with you how I believe they made their contribution to the creation of Affirmative Prayer.

Phinneas Quimby (1802-1866).

Dr. Holmes says of Quimby:

"Probably more than on the work of any other one person, the New Thought Movement of America has been built upon the teachings of Phineas Quimby, who was born in New Hampshire in 1802 and passed from this plane in the state of Maine in 1866. This man was one of the few original thinkers of the ages…Quimby laid his chief emphasis on spiritual mind healing, rather than on the control of conditions through the creative power of thought. He claimed that disease is but a dream from which one may be awakened. His method, according to his son, George Quimby, was to 'change the mind of a patient, and disabuse it of its error and establish the truth in its place, which, if done, was the cure.'" Dr. Ernest Holmes

As I read and re-read The Quimby Manuscripts, I was left with the understanding that Quimby supported individuals in healing maladies through re-educating the patient on their understanding of God. He taught what has become known as the Christ Principle, or Divine Love.

The Quimby Manuscript consists of notes Quimby took on patient cases. He quickly learned that much disease, hatred, fear, and discord could be traced back to indoctrinated fundamental religious beliefs of sin taught by ministers who didn't know the Love of God.

The second source of much illness, he was quick to realize was the doctor whose job it was to find something wrong with a patient through diagnosis and then educate them on the malady until they thoroughly believed it. Once the error of thinking was identified, he would share the Spiritual Truth with the patient and they could become well.

"My practice for twenty years has put me in possession of facts that have opened my eyes to the misery of mankind, from ignorance of ourselves. My object is to correct the false ideas and strengthen the truth. I make war with what comes in contact with health and happiness, believing that God made everything good, and if there is anything wrong it is the effect of ourselves, and that man is responsible for his acts and even his thoughts. Therefore it is necessary that man should know himself so that he shall not communicate sin or error." Phinneas Quimby

Quimby saw himself like a seasoned attorney taking a client's story of how they perceive life and then advocating against their perception until they realized their innate Wholeness. He often used parables as they speak not only to the conscious, but also the unconscious mind. He saw his work as undoing often generations of incorrect thinking.

Emma Curtis Hopkins (1849–1925).

Referred to as the teacher of teachers, Hopkins taught those who would go on to bring forth the New Thought movement in America. She taught Dr. Holmes who founded Science of Mind along with Myrtle and Charles Fillmore who started The Unity movement and Fannie B. James, the founder of the Divine Science Church.

Emma taught the mystical teachings of Truth, had her own private practice of healing others through aligning with The Truth. According to Dr. Holmes, *"She had a high degree of Cosmic Consciousness which one could feel."* Hopkins teachings lean heavily upon the idea of God as All without opposition. She says, *"Another name for God is Good"* and taught from the power of The One Good God.

"Why do we say, 'My Good is my God?' Can we not see that every move we make is to get some good to ourselves? Do we not breathe because we think it will be better for us? If you wish to stop breathing, even that will be because you think it more comfortable not to breathe. You feel deeply that there is Good for you, so all the time you do your best to get that Good. It make the Good your governor. It makes it the governor of your life. Thus it is your God! It is for you to choose to make your God either the most high principle which Jesus Christ taught, or the incidents and happenings of your everyday lot in life. Whatever draws you toward it, making you think it can satisfy you governs you, and is your Good." Emma Curtis Hopkins

My understanding of the Good of God came about from studying the works of Hopkins. She says that Good of God is what each of us seeks; and that we ought to have or possess this Good which we've believed to be separate from us. She said, *"you are your idea of God."* This aligns beautifully with the intention of affirmative prayer.

In Hopkins' writings she speaks often of treatment as connecting with a quality of God and then affirming Truth and denying that which isn't true.

"All science has affirmation and negation. In the science of numbers you subtract what is not wanted from what is wanted. In the science of geology you say, 'This is not aqueous rock, this is not igneous rock.' You show as much wisdom by negation as by

your affirmation." Emma Curtis Hopkins

Non-truths or thoughts of error all share the same root: belief in sin, sickness, or death. Each one of these three belief structures suppress the ability to live the Good life, promised by God, and leave individuals feeling victimized. Believing in sin means believing there is a right and a wrong. This belief sets up conditional thinking. The belief in sickness as a power other than God means the belief in lack of wellbeing that creates an ever-increasing atmosphere of more lack. Lastly, the belief that death is a Reality is contrary to all mystical teachings of life everlasting and looks to visible evidence solely for life's meaning. This belief can set up an avoidance to living fully for fear of loss.

Treatment, then, to Hopkins, is an eradication of this false belief system through affirming the Truth of God and then behaving out of the Truth.

Frederick L. Rawson (1859-1923)

Rawson was a London engineer, businessman, and avid learner. Christian Science was burgeoning in the 1880s and he was asked by The London Daily Mail to research the cult and expose their errors. To do this he began studying Christian Science and came to believe strongly in its claims. He left the church, not wanting to adhere to organizational requirements, and branched out on his own teaching Scientific Prayer. He started the Society for Studying the Knowledge of True Prayer. He had a private practice as a prayer healer with undisputable results. He authored three books: The Nature of True Prayer, Treatment or Healing by True Prayer and Life Understood from a Scientific and Religious Point of View.

Rawson believed prayer to be complete communion with God. Since God is Good, he would say any belief in matter or humanity separate from God would be the belief in evil or devilish thoughts. It is the belief in these ideas as having power independent and separate from God which is what prayer remedies. He suggests a minimum of fifteen minutes of prayer twice a day and acknowledges he invested upward of four hours a day in prayer, when required. Prayer to him was a shifting of thought from the realm of duality back to the Oneness of God, or Heaven. This regular, consistent, on-going practice, he said, would deepen one's consciousness of God.

Rawson identifies four benefits or results of praying affirmatively. First, he says, one learns spiritual discernment, often referred to as judgment in the Bible. Second, by seeing rightly we are able to bring forth a healing atmosphere and watch others benefit from our connection with God the

Good. Third, we can deliver ourselves and others out of precarious situations by shifting our thought from one of sin to God. He quotes the scripture passage *"Seek ye first the Kingdom of God"* as the promise. And fourth, as a regular practitioner of prayer, eventually the inner world takes on the qualities of Heaven and Peace is realized.

"It is evident that the basis of true prayer must be Scientific Right Thinking, as prayer is entirely a matter of what one thinks or realizes." F.L. Rawson

What is Affirmative Prayer?

☑ Affirmative Prayer is a five-step process that begins with connecting with a quality of God until the energy of this quality is evident. Similar to contemplation or centering prayer, the practitioner sits with a Quality or Essence ascribed to God until they feel Truth in their being. Then one recognizes their Oneness with The All and speaks affirmations and denials in order to align one's earthly or dualistic thinking with Spiritual Truth. Gratitude is experienced and the Affirmative Prayer is released.

☑ The intention of affirmative prayer is to *become* and *live from* more of the Presence of the Undifferentiated Go(o)d of God. It can be used to heal, recognize Wholeness, and manifest, yet at its deepest intent it is to viscerally know and experience the Presence of God.

☑ This prayer technology is used by professional Religious Science Practitioners with clients to affirm the Go(o)d beyond mental patterning. Prayer sessions include an interview, similar to that which was done by Phinneas Quimby to identify errors in thinking. The Affirmative Prayer, or treatment, is then spoken as part of the session.

☑ Affirmative Prayer is also called "Spiritual Mind Treatment;" recognizing the preponderance of dis-ease originates within the subjective mind. As a doctor prescribes medication to "treat" a symptom, a metaphysician uses words of Truth from the Spiritual realm for treating the mental "thought" condition.

☑ A regular Affirmative Prayer practice retrains thinking away from worldly indoctrination back to Original Thought or God.

"Man will deliver himself from sickness and trouble in exact proportion to his discovery of himself and his true relationship with the Whole." Dr. Ernest Holmes

Reverend Bonnie

Notes:

CHAPTER 2
PREPARATION

"Prayer, then, is communion, and this communion pronounces life to be Good."
Dr. Ernest Holmes

A Bit More About Me

My desire to become a minister never waned. I attended the Episcopal church weekly through my childhood and often attended church services with my friends, visiting Presbyterian, Congregational, and Baptist church services. In high school I fell in love with languages and went to Spain to study Spanish. Upon my return home, I decided to become a United Nations Interpreter. In college I studied Spanish, German, French, Mandarin Chinese. Then the summer between my sophomore and junior years my parents divorced. I was shattered. My parents were the first in our community to divorce and I didn't know how to navigate the intense pain. Determined to do whatever I could to extricate myself from the home environment, I met with my minister and chose to go on a mission.

I chose to go to Americus Georgia and build houses for Habitat for Humanity. I experienced many firsts that summer. Americus, Georgia and Seattle, Washington are worlds apart from each other in personality. Each afternoon at about 3 pm I could expect a thunder and lightening storm to refresh the muggy morning heat. I would experience more thunder and lightening in that one summer than I had collectively in the decades I'd lived in Seattle. Storms were so rare in Seattle, when they happened, I would be with our family dog hovered under the bed convinced it was the end of world. Praying, crying, repenting, and gritting my teeth through it all, the rarity frightened me. In Georgia, I found the frequency comforting.

I faced many of my fears head-on. I saw my first rat in the center of the street, dead, one morning when jogging. I stood over this flattened ball of fur in amazement at its size. I also saw my first cock roach, which fascinated me. To wake up in the middle of the night and turn on the light and see an entire world in a flurry to then hide from *their* fear of me; amused me. I had to know more about them, so I went to the library and blew up a photograph from the encyclopedia and placed it on the refrigerator with a list of cockroach benefits. Top of the list: they ate bed bugs. I learned that summer to welcome the unknown with curiosity.

I saw racism up close and personal, which was odd to me as one of my best friends in high school was African American. I didn't realize Seattle was progressive as I was living in it. I attended many events where I was one of the only white people in attendance. I learned to be comfortable with standing out and being visibly different.

I made my first hospital visit to a dying woman. Our team was building her a Habitat house, which she would never see. The house building process started prior to her illness, and her husband would move into their new home without her. He wanted me to meet her. I sat with her, prayed with her, and listened to her speak about her life as it was coming to an end.

I took it upon myself to explore different denominations and faiths. I went to church at least twice in a week, giving me more than twenty church experiences that summer. I participated in tent revivals, attended a small, outback country church where snake handling was practiced. I went to Second Baptist Church of Plains where Jimmy Carter was my Sunday School teacher. As he taught, secret service agents were on either side of him and when he called on me, I actively prayed my answer was correct. I went without make up, dressed in white, with a cover on my head sitting in the women's section of the Mennonite Church. The Episcopal church in town had a blind minister. The Sunday I attended he got up for the homily to announce he could say nothing as his faith had dried up and he was bereft. He apologized and the service continued.

I returned from Georgia to Seattle with my heart still broken, lost, and yet having made a contribution despite myself. My desire to become a minister was in full gear, and I changed my studies to Religious Studies where I studied all major world religions. With this study my concept of God became less abstract and distant as I saw Universal themes arising across belief systems. I no longer wanted to be only a "Christian." I wanted to be an All-Faith/No Faith person. I wanted a spiritual life. Despite experiencing the Episcopal teachings as limited, upon graduation I met with my minister to request going to seminary. He wisely told me the church changed its requirement in the 1980s to include life experience as part of its application process. He told me to go out and live. Learn to pay bills, make money, deal with conflict, get scraped up a bit, and then return in my 30s with a lived faith. I had been given my charge.

I found Science of Mind several years later. My first Sunday in church the minister quoted from The Bible, The Koran, The Sutras, The Science of Mind text and a passage from a book on quantum physics. This interfaith approach reminded me of college, the minister was a beautiful woman in a business suit and so I related to her personally, and the music was the best I'd heard in a church environment.

I jumped into studies right away and for the next four years learned how to use Affirmative Prayer for myself and for others. I became a Professional Religious Science Practitioner, which meant I was qualified to meet with individuals and teach spiritual principles while using Affirmative Prayer. Once I passed a written and oral test, I began my private practice, eventually opening an office in the Seattle area where I worked with mostly two populations; those wanting to get healed from a physical issues and entrepreneurs interested in growing their businesses.

I have been teaching and working with clients now for about fifteen years and during this time I have learned a lot about Affirmative Prayer and its Power. I have discovered the preparation for prayer as well as the "after prayer" are just as important as the actual prayer itself.

Preparing for Affirmative Prayer

"There is power in clarity." Rev. Dr. Bonnie Barnard

"Every phenomenon in the natural world has its birth in the spiritual world."
Phinneas Quimby

Psychologists say that we are motivated by pain and pleasure. Rev. Dr. Michael Beckwith says we are either pushed toward The Presence by pain or pulled into It through a vision.

My prayer life, then, falls basically into four categories:

1. Praying for myself out of an experience of pain to be reconciled with Truth. I called these prayers of repair.
2. Praying for myself in order to manifest a desire. Desires, for me, tend to be Soul nudging me toward my vision.
3. Praying for another with their knowledge and agreement.
4. Praying as a form of communion, to simply know more of God as me, or to Surrender into and as the One Will.

Most affirmative prayers, in the beginning are prayers of clean up. These prayers have the intention to heal a painful experience or memory, or experience of feeling "done wrong."

Affirmative Prayer for Transforming Pain

I start by knowing that in God there is no pain, no error, no sin, no wrong. My preparation process and prayerful intention is to detach emotionally in order to see the thought patterns which have been running my mind and recreating the same situation over and over again. I begin by sitting in my chair taking total and complete responsibility for the prayer.

My prayer chair is an overstuffed, lavished red and gold Chippendale chair that was a gift from my beloved father. It is tucked into a corner of my master bedroom suite with antique bookshelves directly behind it and a clear glass table to its side. Each morning and evening I sit in this chair journal, meditate, and then pray.

Many spiritual teachers suggest that having a regular place to do spiritual practice builds an energy environment akin to a heavily prayed in church. In addition, the mind is conditioned for a certain type of activity in this location and so entering into the Sweet Spot of Divine Love can become easier through repetition.

Seated, with a journal and pen in my hand, **I own the issue and prayer as mine**. I realize that all religions say that pain or perceived issues come from the fundamental belief in one's separation from God.

"The problem can be solved by bringing God here where He has placed us. No matter what our environment may be, into the mind where God-communication reigns, Heaven must come". Paramahansa Yogananda

If I enter into prayer with an "issue" wanting resolution, then I own it. I own all of it. I identify the issue which is currently up for me and write it down in the first person. *I recognize the perceived issue is mine even though there is someone else in my story as the way I perceive this story comes out of my mind.* I know that my mental patterns are built upon my own experiences and my emotions flow out of the story I tell myself. So, I own it all.

When I place my issue upon another it is called projection and then they have the power over me in my mind. I take back my power by owning my issue. I get clear about what is up for me and write it down. I also realize the issue is not an indication of who I am, it is built upon what I believe, and my beliefs can be changed.

"According to your faith be it done unto you." Matthew 9:29

F.L. Rawson says he begins first by working the evil (that which isn't God) out of his mind. He calls it a *"method of reversing thought."*

"I myself always start by working against universal evil, called the mortal mind." F.L. Rawson

Story of Transforming Pain Using Affirmative Prayer

I had provided myself with a deadline to complete a book I'd been in the process of writing for two years. To do this, I set aside time each day for uninterrupted writing. This designated time meant I could reach my goal and I was intent on doing this.

An hour into my writing, the phone rings. I don't look at the receiver to see who is calling, I simply pick it up without thinking. On the end of the phone line is an individual with a problem who wants me to listen, solve, or hold the High Watch for him as he walks me through his issue. In other words, he wants me to drop everything I'm doing and provide him a practitioner session without charge.

This assumption has gone with the territory of being a prayer practitioner and a minister. People assume, *"prayer is free"* and ministers do their work out of love. Yes, prayer is free, and I LOVE to do it. I ask for compensation for my time when I work one-on-one with individuals.

So I pick the phone up and the caller launches into his problem with drama, zest, and zeal. He wants to be heard and validated and wants prayer support immediately. I want to write my book.

I listen to him begrudgingly. I want to stop him and yet I was unable to interrupt his momentum; he was on a roll. As his story continues, I become anxious and resentful as I haven't stopped him and requested a session for a later date, or rescheduled the conversation as a gift. He asks me what he can do to ease his pain. I pray with him and hang up. I am aware I didn't come from a loving space. I resented him. Our phone call ends. I allowed this distraction and I felt myself becoming more internally heated. I am filled with funky feelings.

My human mind is wanting to blame him for being inconsiderate. I know, however, I am responsible, and take responsibility for the entire interaction. Recognizing there is no time and space in God, I know I will pray to clean up the internal emotional funk and then pray for him, sincerely, from love.

The preparation for treatment, then, is to become clear about how I have hindered the flow of God, or as Emma Curtis Hopkins would say Good, in my life. I do this by sitting in my prayer chair and creating an action flow chart based upon the choices I made.

Action 1: I Visually Chart My Choice Points.

In the above story I have five decision points, possible more. I take a piece of paper and create a flow chart so I can visually see the action.

First, I *choose* to make my *book important*.

Second, I *choose* to *answer* the phone.

Third, I *categorized* this person as non-client, a needy taker.

Forth, I *choose* to *listen*.

Fifth, I *choose* to *label* the energy within me *funky*.

Disassembling the story into a flow chart allows me to see my behavior independent of the story I've created. It is my pattern on paper. I sit with it and feel into it a bit. As I do this I often receive information such as the frequency or longevity of the pattern, if it was inherited and from who or where. Any and all insights I receive, serve me.

I am aware that if I had made a different choice at any of these junctures, my perception of the interaction would have been different. Had my book not been important to me, then the call may have been welcomed. Had I chose not to answer the phone, then I could have checked the message at a convenient time for myself and managed my time in a different way. I could have answered the phone, and immediately suggested an appointment at a later time when he could receive more attention. Each step altered would have changed the outcome. This is great information for future similar situations.

This wisdom alone was worth the phone call with the funky residue.

Now for the inner feeling tone of funk. I get real with myself. This funk has nothing to do with the caller and everything to do with me not keeping my commitment to myself of uninterrupted writing time. Because of this I diminished another person, making him and the situation wrong.

This is a MONUMENTAL insight. I didn't honor my work as a writer or a professional practitioner. *I didn't value me.* Yet, what I saw was the caller wasn't valuing me. Interesting.

I look at the false belief system which I was engaged in – it was the belief in *lack of value.* Lack of time. Lack of boundaries. Lack of knowledge, known as ignorance. I believed, in addition to God, in an energy which I label as not-enoughness or Lack.

My perceived issue, as I enter into prayer, is the making of right/wrong (judgment), the belief in lack (time and value) and operating out of integrity with myself. This was the funky feeling I experienced.

Action #2: Identify the Quality of God as Remedy

Once I've charted out the action and identified the underlying belief, my next step in preparation is to **Identify the quality of God wanting to come forward**. Sometimes the quality is obvious and yet I sit with the energy of the insight until I am certain of the quality which wants to be known within me based upon the perceived issue at hand.

Using the above example of healing lack, judgmental responsiveness, being out of integrity with myself, and missing the gift in the conversation, I identify the quality of God which would be restorative as Grace. Grace of self, Grace of other, Grace of situation, Grace of insight. I am wanting a dose or two of Grace. I could have chosen Abundance or Generosity, but Grace felt right when I sat with it.

If I am experiencing a health challenge, I may pray to know the quality of God as Wholeness.

If I can't see work and I am wanting to express my gifts and talents, I may pray to know the Expressive Givingness of God as me.

If I am believing in lack, I may choose to know God as Abundant Wealth. I can step into the Field of God as plenty of time, money, resources, etc.

If I yearn for friendship or an intimate relationship, I pray to know God as Love in the here and now.

Action #3: Become Grounded/Centered in The Body

I have my story choice points identified, I am clear about the pattern of thought that was in operation and the underlying belief at work, and I have selected the restorative quality of God identified, **I turn my attention to my body and I do whatever it takes to ground and center my body prior to prayer.**

Unhealed grief and trauma creates a fracture within the emotional body which often leads to an energetic separation between the emotional self and the physical self. This shows up as not being home inside of one's body. With trauma the emotional body becomes jarred and can live above one's head or to the side of one's physical body.

Unhealed trauma is fairly common and I have known my share of it. This is what I've come to know through the practice of Affirmative Prayer: if I am praying from a fractured self without my emotional body in communication with my physical body, then my prayer to become more of God as me is extremely difficult. Prayer, when I'm centered is felt, known, realized, and embodied quickly.

Prayer depends upon my ability to feel/know Reality as High Truth and to align my splintered, dualist, temporary thoughts with The Eternal.

When I come from this fractured place, I am in my thinking mind and speaking rote without engaging my heart, feeling the energy within my body and experiencing a full-bodied prayer. It has become a part of my regular prayer practice to ensure I am *in my body fully intact*. When I work with a client, I lead them through grounding exercises before we enter into the field of prayer so the two of us enter into it Whole together.

Consciously integrating the body, mind, heart, and emotions allows for Spiritual Treatment, or Affirmative Prayer, to operate powerfully.

Practices for Centering Within My Body

☑ I take a walk feeling my feet touching the earth and acknowledging the solid ground feeling to myself. I may do like the Buddhists and with each step whisper to myself "step, step, step."

☑ I engage in brain gym activities. These tend to integrate both sides of the body, creating a centering experience.

☑ I practice some basic yoga stretches or poses. I enjoying stretching and affirming simultaneously.

☑ I practice mindfulness by orienting myself through my senses to the present environment.

☑ I become aware of what I'm smelling, tasting, seeing, kinesthetically feeling, and emoting at the moment. Stepping into the present now aligns my body beautifully.

☑ I apply lotion consciously to my body awake to the movement of my hand and the sensation of the lotion, or I shower consciously feeling the water pelting upon my skin.

☑ In a meditative pose, I feel my body seated within my prayer chair and feel my feet touching the ground, my back up against the chair's body and my butt against the cushion. I practice feeling all three simultaneously.

☑ I tap my head region, my heart/chest area, and then my belly, feeling the tapping and the skin being tapped simultaneously.

☑ I place my attention upon and follow my breath within my body. I feel it moving throughout my body as an inner massage.

Action #4: I Assess for and Practice Forgiveness

I remain honest with myself and identify if any **forgiveness or blessing** needs to take place prior to stepping into affirmative prayer. Jesus mentions this throughout his ministry. Here is one quote:

"And when ye stand praying, forgive, if ye have ought against any: that your Father also which is in heaven may forgive you your trespasses." Mark 11:15

I think of the example I used in this chapter about praying to embody or know the Grace of God. If I am holding a grudge against who I perceive to be another, I am the holder of the grudge. To receive Grace, I must first give it. So, I sit and make a list of who is to receive my blessing/forgiveness.

As an empath, I typically feel people's energy upon meeting. I tend to know people through feeling their energetic presence. This has allowed me to know people as packages of energy or presence more than personality or presentation. The beauty of this is I realize I am not forgiving or blessing a person as much as I transforming my own energy in response to my perception of another's energy. Forgiveness for me is moving from judgment into Love.

"The potential for forgiveness exists within the energy dynamic of right and wrong. In this dynamic someone is right or innocent and someone is wrong or guilty. Forgiveness is the bringing forth of Love to transform this dynamic."
Rev. Dr. Bonnie Barnard

Ways I incorporate forgiveness into my practice:

☑   I dedicate or include within my prayer someone I've placed outside of my heart. As I pray that I may know, feel, understand, give and receive the Grace of God, I know this for anyone who I perceive to be an enemy or of contrary energy. This is one active form of for-giving or giving forth.

☑   I may choose a visualization and see the other in my mind's eye, surrounded in light and happy and then releasing them from my mental space.

☑   I speak words of *blessing* and *gratitude* for the Good developing within me and recognizing there is only One of us here.

☑   I may cradle and rock another in my mind as a mother holds a child. I may see them surrounded with all of the blessings I can imagine from great health to abundant wealth and to peace of mind. As I rock the two of us, I experience myself as the Divine Mother and the innocent child. Sometimes I'm guided to switch positions with the person I'm rocking so they become the Divine Mother and I assume the innocent child.

Once I am in my body and energetically clean, I am ready for Affirmative Prayer.

The Preparation Process in Review

☑   Identify the Pattern of Disturbance with a flow chart.

☑   Feel into the quality of God which is the remedy.

☑   Become centered and grounded within the body.

☑   Purify the mind through forgiveness.

Reverend Bonnie

Notes:

CHAPTER 3
STEP ONE: RECOGNITION

"Every great spiritual teacher has known God as One--not two."
Dr. Ernest Holmes

"The pantheistic doctrine of the Gita is that God is everything."
Paramahansa Yogananda

"You were born of God. You go toward God. You know God.
You have the power of God." Emma Curtis Hopkins

The first step of treatment is hanging out in the knowing that *God is all there is.* There is nothing other than God. There is not God *and* any opposite force; simply God. God is It. The Alpha and the Omega, the beginning and the end and everything in between, God is the Unmanifest and the manifest. God is. Metaphysicians have determined all problems, illness, experiences of limitation, are born out of the belief in two opposing powers. Beginning, then in the recognition of The One is the solution and start of all treatment.

Knowing Oneness, I sit with the quality of God I am desiring to know more deeply. Using the previous example of Grace, I sit in the energy of The Unerring, Ever-present Giving forth of Love beyond condition. I begin my prayer by recognizing and feeling into this state of consciousness. In this state, I experience the Abundance and Sufficiency or Unlimited Nature of God which is the natural remedy to my perception of lack.

When I first began my Affirmative Prayer process I wrote my prayers down so I could practice the five step process, could see what I have written, and could speak my prayer out loud and consciously experience the resonance within and behind the words.

I limit myself to one aspect of God. Instead of the kitchen sink approach of throwing all words or qualities of God into a prayer, I commit to nurturing a singular aspect of God which my Soul wants to develop.

Emma Curtis Hopkins said, *"Another name for God is Good."* We are always seeking our Good. By Divine Birthright; the Presence of Undifferentiated Good is All Present and always present. In this first step of Affirmative Prayer, I am recognizing the quality of God I wish to embody more of as I speak the Truth and I feel the energy of the words spoken.

"God is another name for infinite intelligence. To achieve anything in life, a piece of this intelligence must be contacted and used. In other words, God is always there for you."
Deepak Chopra

In Recognition, I remind myself of the Oneness of God and identify the quality of God I wish to know more of. I recognize the Allness and Only of God and pray *from* this knowing. I don't pray *to* God, I pray *from* the Consciousness of God.

The Creation Process

Life begins with God. It is the Alpha and the Omega. It is The All and the Only. God, then, is individualized and takes form as The Living. Within each form of life is the Presence of God wearing different outward shells. We start in the Invisible realm of God, we take on physical form and our Essence, Energy, Life Force is the Presence of God. When we die, we drop our physical bodies returning to the Invisible.

"Do you not know you are temple of the Holy Spirit who is within you, whom you have received from God? You are not your own." 1 Corinthians 6:19

Although the Presence indwells each of us, in order for It to become predominate, It must be given permission or welcomed. This is done by becoming more in alignment with It through living out Its Nature as Love, Beauty, Intelligence, Joy, Givingness, and so forth.

I mentioned in the previous chapter the four uses of Affirmative Prayer. We looked in Chapter 2 at prayer for healing or restoring erroneous beliefs back to Truth. The second reason I gave for prayer

is for the fulfillment of desire. The word de-sire, literally means *Of the Father.*

Desire is deeper than temporary earthly pleasure, it is a yearning within the Soul which wants to be known. It is often aligned with one's life vision, and yet sometimes shows up without a direct identifiable correlation. I call these *mystery yearnings*, following the clues. Either way, Affirmative Prayer is a powerful force for fulfilling desires or creating out of a vision.

Story of Using Affirmative Prayer for Fulfilling a Desire

A client of mine has a thriving professional service business. The lease on her current building was coming to an end and the rental climate had changed dramatically. Corporate rentals, which once were scarce, were now plentiful, with many sitting vacant.

She found an office space twice the size of her current one for half of the price and she walked into it loving it right away. In order to secure the lease she would need a deposit, which she didn't currently have in her account. She had plenty of money on its way to her, it just wasn't liquid at that moment.

Our session together was to pray for the fulfillment of her best work done in the most optimal space for her grateful clients while having all of the resources necessary in order to make this happen.

Together, we sat in the energy of the Sufficiency and Overflow of God. We touched upon the agreement of God as All. God as The Divine Idea and the manifest form. All of it. We reveled in her love of the office. Not from a place of attachment, but from the knowing that God is Love and when we experience Love, we are knowing God.

The following day she received a phone call from the landlord suggesting she pay the deposit in installments. Done. She moved in within two weeks.

Step One: Recognizing God

The first step of Affirmative Prayer is to begin where it all begins; in, with, and from God.

Step 1: Recognition
God is All There is. I identify one quality of God.

Qualities of God are agreed upon qualities of Good which are ascribed to the One Presence. These qualities are spoken of in holy scriptures. I am providing a partial list of God-qualities. The more they are contemplated, integrated into daily living, identified and cultivated, the more energy and subtleties they will reveal. I provide this list and definitions as I've come to know them.

Qualities of God

Good. The Good of God has no opposite. It could be called Divine or Eternal Good. It is the word spoken in Genesis after creation took place and *"It was Good."* God said *"let there be light, and there was light. And God saw that the light was good."* (Genesis 1:3) Knowing God as the Undivided quality of Good is knowing a state of undisputable satisfaction.

Joy. Joy is the potency of Spirit, it is considered the fruit of Spirit or evidence of Its Presence. Where joy resides, God is in Full recognition. To know Joy is to know the Energy of "The Uplift." *"Rejoice with great splendor for God has made you the Day Spring of his light."* (Baha'u'llah and the New Era, 237)

Abundance. Also known as the energy of plenty, enoughness, or Wealth; Abundance is the recognition that the Life of God is an expansive one. It is the energy of a seed becoming a tree and populating an orchard. It is the worlds without end consciousness. It is Unlimited by Nature. *"Out of abundance, he took abundance, and abundance still remained."* (The Upanishads) Knowing the Abundance of God is knowing the multiplying factor of God's Good.

Faith. Faith is the energy of certainty without visible proof. It is a cultivated Spirit; a strong intuitive knowing; a vivid conviction of the Power of the Invisible. *"Whatever his faith is, he is."* (Bhagavad Gita v 17) Living Faith is living proactively and inspired.

Peace. Peace is an inner state of calm despite appearances. It is an internal firmament of conviction. Peace is not passive, but powerfully regenerative. *"Peace comes from the absence of fear, from a consciousness of trust, from a deep underlying faith in the absolute goodness and mercy, the final integrity of the universe in which we live, and of every cause to which we live, and of every cause to which we give our thought, our time and our attention."* (Dr. Ernest Holmes) To come from the Peace of God is to come from Unwavering wellbeing.

Love. Divine Love is the strongest energy/power in existence. It changes, transforms, heals, reveals, up-levels, softens what it touches. To be in the presence of an individual who actively embodies this energy can render one speechlessness and create palpable vibrational shifts in the body. Having been touched by or embodied Divine Love leaves the evidence of feeling like being home, experiencing a Safety/Trust uncommon to ordinary consciousness, feeling deeply understood, seen, and accepted. To come from the Love of God is to embody the energy of the Prodigal Son's father.

Infinite. The consciousness of The Infinite is the consciousness of *without end.* It is a timeless consciousness which transcends and includes the present moment. Coming from The Infinite is coming from Right Action, Right Words, Right Disposition. It is clean and pure. It is That which is beyond the ego's perception of life and death. To know The Infinite is to know Ultimate Freedom.

Health. Another word for Health is Wholeness or Holiness. It is the realization that nothing is wrong in the body or body of affairs. It is the honoring of the innate Perfection within all embodied forms of Life. It is the indwelling recognition of the Innocence and Purity of God. *"Man is not a material being, liable to sin, disease, and trouble of every kind, but that he is a perfect being in heaven, in Christ."* (F.L. Rawson)

Substance. Substance is the shared Life Force from which all Life is created. It is the Being Nature out of which doing or creation emerges. To know Substance is to know the Energetic Fabric of Becoming. *"Meditating upon Substance eradicates fear."* (Rev. Dr. Bonnie Barnard) *"Curving back upon itself, I create again and again."* (Bhagavad Gita, Chapter 9:8)

Power. Power is the recognition that the Center of God is everywhere.

"The power of God is with you at all times; through activities of mind, senses, breathing, and emotions; and is constantly doing all the work using you as a mere instrument." (Bhagavad Gita) It is utilized in thought through the words yes, know, and the exercise of persistent commitment. It is the energy of *"standing."* Standing in, standing from and standing with.

Creative. In the beginning; God. As we cultivate and become more of the Creative Nature of God, we realize we are crafting, re-creating, or co-creating, channeling, or Being. These are all various stages in consciousness related to creativity. There is One Creator, just as there is One Light, One Life, One Truth, and One Good. Knowing God as creativity is to become a High form of service to humanity.

Light. Light is the Intelligence of God in a vibrational form. It is coded communication between one another. Within the Light is healing and reparative energy, direct wisdom, and power. *"There is a light that shines beyond all things on earth, beyond the highest, the very highest heavens. This is the light that shines in your heart."* (The Upanishads)

Life (force). *"I am the way, and the truth, and the life. No one comes to the Father but through me."* John 14:16. This scripture indicates the way to living, becoming alive, embodying life is through activating the consciousness of Christ within you. Life is Christ consciousness. It is the consciousness of an easy yolk, a beloved parentage, an everlasting Soul, a givingness of Spirit and a miracle doer. Life comes through knowing the inner Christ as the very Beingness I am. Praying to know Life is praying that my I am is The I Am and then acting out of It.

Beauty. Beauty is everywhere present. Almost without definition. To see the beauty in all of life conditions is to be free from the lure of the condition. To know Beauty is to have the sight of God. *"If you permit yourself to dwell on evil, you yourself will become ugly. Look only for the good in everything so you absorb the quality of beauty."* (Paramahansa Yogananda)

Supply. Supply is knowing that which is needed is always provided; often in advance. To know the Supply of God is to embody deep Trust in the Givingness of God.

Perfection. Perfection is another word for Holiness. When one realized the Perfection of God, blessing is the natural evidence. Perfection is the embodiment of the All is Well, All is Good, Let it Be consciousness. *"Be perfect, therefore, as your heavenly Father is perfect."* (Matthew 5:48)

Prosperity. To know Prosperity is to know I am the richness of God. Within me lies of the Power of the Presence. I cannot be harmed or endangered, I am innately Prospered and deeply loved. It is the consciousness of filling up and spilling over.

Truth. The early metaphysicians realized something powerful. People were sick, miserable, tired, and unhappy because they believed in lies of man which were often called evil or demons. The Spiritual Truth (thus the capital T), would reverse the thinking and the conditions would change. Truth, is a proven Power of God. To embody Truth means to know Spiritual Truth Principles and to live from them until they begin living you. Truth is a way of being, speaking, and acting in the world. *"Then you will know the truth, and the truth will set you free."* (John 8:32)

Trust. To know the Trust of God is to know that everything works together for my good, despite my perception of it. Trust is being on Team God and coming from Soul Integrity within all interactions. The consciousness of Infinity and Trust share tight bonds.

Writing Your Step One of Affirmative Prayer

In Chapter 2, Preparation, we looked at an issue to bring into prayer for shifting our perception. In this chapter we looked at a desire as the starting point of prayer. Now it is your turn. Ready?

Begin with your perceived problem or desire:

Now ask yourself, if I were to know this quality of God as alive within me, which one would transform or heal your issue? Or, what is yearning within you to be known?

Now that you are clear on the quality. We will begin with the Oneness of God and move to your quality. Affirmative Prayer is to be spoken not from a place of inquiry or petition, but from a place of knowing. I sometimes start my prayers with "I know that ..."

Feel free to borrow some of my examples as you get started.

Example 1: God is All there Is. There is not God AND anything; there is God AS everything. God is the Good which I seek. God is (insert quality here).

Example 2: The mystics have said that All there Is, is God. There is nothing other than this Presence. It is Omnipresent. There is nothing outside of Its knowingness; It is Omniscient. There is no dual power; God is Omnipotent. God is It.

Example 3: I sit down today in prayer, beginning at the beginning. In the beginning, God. In the beginning, God. In the beginning, God. And as every moment is new; every moment is a beginning. I begin in the Consciousness of God, I begin in the consciousness of Good as (insert quality here).

Example 4: I know God Is. God is Peace. God is the Undivided, Whole, Peace.

Example 5: God is One. God is (*insert quality here*).

Example 6: God is All there Is. God is (*insert quality here*).

Example 7: There is One Life. And that Life is God's Life and It is (*insert quality here*).

Example 8: God is All there Is. There is no opposite to God. There is One Life, and It is Infinite. It is All. It is Everlasting. It is without end. God is. As God is It, I sit in the Consciousness today of God as (*insert quality here*).

"*In starting a Treatment it is a great thing to think about God in his various aspects. Think, therefore of God as inexhaustible perfect Love; incorporeal everlasting Life; and ever-present Omnipotent Truth, unfolding its own immortal ideas; as self-existent, unfathomable Mind, which gives all the mental activity in heaven; divine and sinless Soul, which gives all the wonderful wisdom and knowledge that real man has; supreme infinite Spirit, which is the cause of all goodness and holiness (remember that holiness means wholeness or perfection); divine substance which gives permanence to everything in the spiritual world; the unerring and only intelligence; and last, but not least, as Principle, the Principle of peace, joy, harmony, energy, activity, the Principle of law and order, and the Principle of all the many qualities which, with the main eight qualities already mentioned, make up absolute good, known as God.*" F.L. Rawson

WARNING

A mistake some individuals make is to bring earthly, manifest ideas into the first step. Train yourself NOT to do this. The first step is about BEING in the Unified Field of God's Good; it is not about channels or evidence of It; that comes later.

An example of this error would be referring to God is All there is and equating God to puppy dogs, rainy days, flowers blooming. God is NOT these forms; God shows up as these forms. God is Eternal Life and It shows up as embodied life in the form of puppy dogs, raining days, etc. God is Love and shows up as friends and partners. From the Consciousness of the Invisible; to form the visible.

Step One is referred to as "Recognition" as it recognizes The All of God, The Only of God, The Undivided Nature of God, as the one quality you've chosen to intimately cultivate.

Recognition is referred to as the most powerful of all steps within Affirmative Prayer. This is because once I have Recognized the Allness of God/The Allness of Good, then the power around the perceived issue dissipates. Allow yourself the opportunity to wallow in the Nature of Oneness. To sit in the energy of It.

"The new patterns of belief must be found in higher consciousness."
Dr. Ernest Holmes

"True prayer is thinking of God, conscious communion with God." F.L. Rawson

"The first step in Spiritual Mind Treatment may be framed as if it was in answer to questions such as these: What do I know about Spirit? Is Spirit truly all there is? Can you see Spirit in all things? Does the entire universe dwell within the Oneness of Spirit? The stronger your statement of recognition, the more powerful the result will be; the more ambiguous the statement, the less effective your Treatment will be."
Rev. John Waterhouse

INSIGHT

As I pray from the Oneness of God, it is as though I am reaching up in the invisible realm and switching my internal radio dial from Station Duality to Station Oneness. All problems exist in the realm of form which is the realm of opposites. Duality exists within the senses.

Faith is going beyond the visible seen world into a Higher Resonance; the Only Resonance, God. As I begin prayer, I may repeat myself many times over. Repetition is one of the ways I train my mind. I am "going upstairs" from my limited, differentiated, problem, individual, consciousness into the Wholeness which does not know problems. I sit until I feel the shift within me from the individual to the Only.

CHAPTER 4
STEP TWO: UNIFICATION

"If God is to interpret himself to man, He must interpret himself through man."
Dr. Ernest Holmes

"Each one of us is an outlet to God and an inlet to God."
Dr. Ernest Holmes

The second step of Affirmative Prayer speaks of my relationship with God. Traditional religion views God as a Deity, separate being, and someone I am to earn favor with and not piss off. Metaphysicians, mystics and believers with direct experiences of the Divine recognize God as a Presence which indwells all of life.

"Everything that Spirit does actualizes in only one of two ways: Spirit expresses and Spirit experiences." Rev. John Waterhouse

Since God is all there is, then I am, by deduction, an expression of the Living God. It must reside within me, I must reside in It. In fact, It must be me. Dr. Holmes often uses the analogy of the ocean. God is the ocean and I am a wave in the ocean. I am not God or the ocean in Its entirety; however, my entire being as a wave of the ocean is God. I am made in Its image and likeness. I have within me the qualities of God as the very being I am.

A more current metaphor would be that of the world wide web. The internet is accessible to everyone and it is the energetic, technological interface which all computers, or individual devices connect from, to, and by it. The internet needs a computer, phone, or device in order to express itself, just as the Presence of God needs each of us in order to experience life directly.

"I and the Father are one." John 10:30

"Jesus said unto them, 'verily, verily I say unto you, before Abraham was, I am." John 8:58

The Power of the I Am Consciousness

"I am with you, in front of you, behind you, and totally encompass you. I am closer to you than your very self.' Quran 20:11f

The story of Moses and the burning bush is essential to understanding the relationship between God and man.

Moses was crossing a field as his attention was drawn to a bush fire which continued to burn, yet wasn't burning itself out. As he approached this bush God began to speak to him, calling him by name; 'Moses, Moses.' Moses responds, 'Here I am God,' and then is instructed to take off his sandals where the ground is recognized as being holy. (God lures and asks, Moses responds, which creates a place of Holiness/Wholeness.)

Moses was given the assignment to free the Israelite slaves from Egypt, a substantial task. When Moses asks God who he ought to say sent him, the response is *"I am that I am. Tell him I am sent you."* Exodus 3:14

Hebrew scholars say the translation of the words *I am* not only represents the singular verb to be, but represents all of the tenses of the word. It includes *always was, always shall be* and *is at this moment.* These words hold within them the energy of the Alpha and Omega, or always.

As I contemplate, then, on the I am nature of God, the energy to me is Omni, or all time and space directional. I am represents the Omnipresence of God.

Recognizing this wakes me up to my own usage of the words *I am.* When I speak of myself as *I am,* I now stop and ask myself, is this a True statement about me? Was it always true, will it always be true, is it true now and is it surround-sound True? Would I say this about God? Would I say this about my beloved daughter or closest friends?

In metaphysics, language is the paramount importance. It symbolically demonstrates a vibrational quality or energy beneath the words spoken. Words call forth and create. The importance of integrity of thought, speech, and aligned behavior is everything.

With this in mind, the words 'I am' are not throw-away words, but invitations into the Great I am of God.

The second step in treatment is called unification. In this step I am recognizing my relationship to God using the words 'I am.' Just as I may identify myself from a biological lineage, I am the daughter of ... I now train myself into linking who I am with the Truth of who I am. Who sent me? I am.

Step Two: Unification

Step 1: Recognition God is All There is. I identify one quality of God.

Step 2: Unification God is. I am.

This second step of Affirmative Recognizes as God is All, then I am unified, or one with The All. Whatever quality I know to be of God, I know to be individualized as me. This step is easy to write and say and incredibility powerful to receive in consciousness.

Here are some examples:
Step 1: God is Love
Step 2: I am love. I am the beloved. I am loved. I love.

Step 1: God is Peace

Step 2: I am the Peace of God. I am peace. I am peaceful. I am expression of Peace. I express the Peace of God I am.

Step 1: God is Ever-Abundant, always giving forth of Itself. Multiplying Good in through and out All Life.
Step 2: I am the abundant nature of God.

Step 1: God is All there Is. God is Wisdom.
Step 2: I am the wisdom of God, I am wise.

Step 1: God is Health, also known as Wholeness.
Step 2: The Wholeness of God is the very fabric of Who and What I am. I am Whole.

The greatest minds of the ages have accepted that such a pattern (Divine Self) exists. Socrates called it his spirit, Jesus his Father in Heaven. Some ancient mystics called it Atman. Why don't you just call it you, your complete self? For surely this is what they all have meant.

Just try to catch the larger vision and realize that there have been and are people, many of them, who have wooed and wed some invisible presence until Its atmosphere and essence have become woven into the fabric of their own existence. Every man is a doorway, as Emerson said, through which the Infinite passes into the finite, through which God becomes man, through which the Universal becomes individual. Dr. Ernest Holmes

Okay, it is your turn. Staying with prayer you began in the last chapter, add step two of affirmative prayer; unification; to the process.

Step One: God is:

Step 2: I am:

Note: There are many names for God. This Presence doesn't care what It is called. Dr. Ernest Holmes referred to It as The Thing Itself. Spirit, Allah, Yahweh, Ram, Om, Presence, The All, are some names that can be tried on in prayer. I use "Divine" or "Infinite" before a quality; such as Divine Love or Infinite Joy. I use The Field of Good often. I like the feel those words provoke within my body. Give yourself permission to play with various names for God.

Prayer now becomes the communion of the lesser with the greater,
which makes it possible for man not to reverse natural law, but to reverse his position in
it in such a way that bondage becomes freedom.
Dr. Ernest Holmes

When the higher transforms into the lower,
it transforms the nature of the lower into that of the higher.
Meister Eckhart

Freedom will come with the understanding of God as Consciousness,
of Consciousness as Omnipresence, and the realization that this
Consciousness is the consciousness of individual man.
Let us never think that freedom will come while we believe that God
is anywhere except omnipresent as the consciousness of individual man. Freedom comes
when we realize our true identity.
Joel Goldsmith

To use the Creative Process, we must Affirm the Creative Power -- that is to say, we
must go back to the Beginning of the series and start with Pure Spirit, only remembering
that this starting-point is now to be found in ourselves, for this is what distinguishes the
individual Creative Process from the cosmic one.
Thomas Troward

Notes:

CHAPTER 5
STEP THREE: REALIZATION

"In treatment, whenever you can put in the word 'infinite,' do so." F.L. Rawson

"We have to constantly remember the inexorable law; that we only bring so much of the kingdom of God into the world as we possess within us." Albert Schweitzer

"How much life can a man experience? As much as he can embody."
Dr. Ernest Holmes

In prayer, you have recognized the Allness of God and quality which when embodied changes who you are in order to become more of your authentic self and grow beyond whatever problem, issue, or pattern you've been unconscious to up until now. Then you unified with the quality of God, knowing as God is; so too are you.

This third step is concrete. I often refer to is as the "therefore step." God is, I am, therefore …

Step One, Recognition, is Universal and true to all. Step Two, Unification, personalizes Truth to me. Step Three, Realization, then brings the consciousness of Heaven to earth. "I am" answers the question, what is my life like now, or who am I now in consciousness, since knowing my oneness with God? I am speaking of the effect of this embodiment within my life.

The practice of building realizations calls us into a Deeper aspect of being and creates within a feeling tone which pulls us toward 'making this prayer real.' I am going for the feeling tone of 'It is Done' and I believe it.

There are some components of Realization that are helpful when writing and speaking them:

1. They are crafted in the present tense.
2. They are about you and your unfoldment, not someone else.
3. Treatment is to be spoken in the first person (I or me).
4. Each prayer has a singular focus in alignment with steps 1 and 2.
5. The Realization is composed of affirmative statements and denials.

Step 1: Recognition
God is All There is. I identify one quality of God.

Step 2: Unification
God is. I am.

Step 3: Realization
Therefore ... I accept, I claim, I know, I realize

Realization is in the Present Tense

In God and in my mind, there is only one active timeframe, which is the NOW moment. It is the present. My affirmative prayer may be a call for a healthy body and my body may be currently overweight and presenting itself as not well. My body represents the culmination of past thinking followed by past actions. My prayer today is about recreation and making new. My consciousness takes place in a timeless realm. My words are spoken in the NOW as if already done and speaking to the current state as complete.

My Affirmative Prayer is About Me

When my daughter moved out of the house to start her life as an adult, I found myself worrying. I worried if she would have enough food, if she would be liked, if she could handle the big city. I found myself afraid. Afraid for her; and, afraid for me. During that week, my session with my prayer practitioner was not about my daughter, or my worry, it was about *me* Trusting God. My prayer, then, became about Trust and my ability to let go of mother anxiety and Trust the I Am of God as me.

When I teach Affirmative Prayer classes, this tends to be one of the most difficult aspects of practice when first beginning. Trust me on this, whatever issue you are dealing with does not have to do with your mother, father, boss, neighborhood association, children, church, it is about you. Your prayer is yours. And this is where your prayer work is to be focused. This is where I find creating the flow chart in Preparation so vital to me. It separates out the people and shows me a pattern which is alive within me.

I Speak in the First Person

The realization is an inner experience and so I speak of myself as I or me. I am .... I let .... I allow .... I see .... I accept .... I know .... I realize .... I embrace .... I don't speak of myself as You as though I am disassociated and speaking to or about me. I own the words and I own the feeling power of them.

My Prayer Has a Singular Focus

If I begin my prayer with the quality of God as Joy, I remain consistent with joy throughout my prayer including the Realization. Unless intuitively moved to open to an aspect of God related to Joy, which can occasionally happen, I stick with my starting quality of God. This generates potency and understanding.

Affirmative Statements

Affirmative Prayer is composed of affirmations and statements of denial. Affirmations are written in the present tense, as if it is done, and is written from the positive. It is a process of speaking Truth as a confirmation and evoking the feeling tone within me of completion. An example of an affirmative realization for health is below:

My body radiates the healthy energy of God's Good. I now recognize the health of God pulsing through each and every vein in my body. My cells scream out the health of God which they are and as they multiply, they multiple this Good. My energy reflects this health, too. I am revitalized and nourished through the Word of Good as I wake up to this prayer as my body, that I may feel and know God within my very body temple. I can feel it now. My health has turned the corner. God's miraculous Good is operating within my being. Perfect assimilation, digestion, and release happens. My body's set point is Health. My body's set point is God.

Outlining a Prayer: This or Something Better

The above prayer does not indicate HOW my body is going to achieve the Health of God. It is sitting in the Health of God speaking from my body knowing that the unfoldment is magical and doesn't require me knowing how or having a plan. This is a big deal. I am not using my mental intelligence to figure it out. I am going beyond my small thinking into the realm of possibility knowing the Infinite Presence of God knows exactly how to unfold my prayer, and I don't need to know how.

However, there are times when I have been given clues to what I desire based upon what I love. The energy of love compels. It beckons life into existence. I may be praying for a home for me to live in and be very clear that gardens bring me joy, or while reading a book by the fireplace I enter into a peaceful state. I may have clues on specific details and yet I don't allow them to limit me as I practice opening to a Greater Good.

In Affirmative Prayer, when I tell my Inner Presence exactly what I desire, I leave space open for a greater, larger, more satisfying result by using the phrase *"this or something better."* I can outline the home I think I'd like in my prayer. I can state the number of rooms, the neighborhood, the price range, etc." What I am (my Soul) really wanting isn't a house, but to lean into God to receive the perfect living for me in my life at this moment. It may not be a "house." It may be a condo, apartment, house sitting while someone is out of town for a year. It may be a castle, an estate, a shared living situation. The form may be even better than what I could imagine, and, the underlying Good as desire is the driver. Here is a sample detailed, outlined, prayer:

I find the perfect right living condition for me, now. I call forth a light and airy space with lots of greenery and windows. I accept a home in a diverse, safe, Phoenix neighborhood with a grocery store within walking distance and a community church nearby. I celebrate the pool I swim in on hot summer days and I enjoy the fruit I eat from the many different trees in my yard. I step into this living space and know immediately the space is mine. I claim a knowing so profound when I see it, I act upon it. I claim the Lilly of the fields consciousness right now. I worry not about how I will be housed, I trust the right housing is finding me as I continue to step toward it. God is my Supply. God is my Good.

Statements of Denials

"All you need to say is yes or no." Matthew 5:37

"You will notice that the instant you acknowledge there is a Good for you which you ought to have, the thought arises within your mind that you do not have the good that belongs to you. You feel that your good is absent from you. This is a universal feeling." Emma Curtis Hopkins

In the above Realization for a healthy body, I may get stuck in my mind believing it is not possible. I may have tried umpteen diets, been to hundreds of doctors, read every book about the body which relates to my symptom and the stretch to believing that my body can be a radiant demonstration of the Good of God, may be just too difficult. Or, as Hopkins says, once I say it is done, the first thing to cross my mind is seeing that it isn't. This is where denials are powerful.

Affirmative Prayer takes place in one's mind and heart. It is accessing what isn't and hasn't been which exists in the Invisible Realm. Looking at the visible realm for verification happens, but it isn't powerful. The power is in the cultivated feeling tone of *It Is Done* and acting from this completed idea. With the example of health, I know it is done within my mind, feel it from my heart, and then I act from the energy of being a person of radiant health.

Affirmative Prayer retrains my mind to think from the Consciousness of God the Good. I am retraining me. The words and the energy behind them must move me in order for me to shift. There are times when I need to bring in a wrecking crew to break up a real hard belief. This is the role of the denial.

41

My body radiates the healthy energy of God's Good. I stop lying to myself right now and quit believing that a book or an external source will somehow change me. I take back my power now and recreate myself from the inside out. I begin in the only place I can begin in; God. God is Health, and I am healthy. I stop lying now and saying I am tired. I no longer believe in the idea I can't. I accept the Power of Who I am right now and this Power shows Itself throughout all of my life, including in my body. I say 'no' to lethargy. I deny the belief that what once was, must always be. I accept my body as vital now.

In the example of the house, I may use the following denials:

I do not give my power to the current state of real estate. God is bigger than this.

I refuse to believe that the Good of God exists everywhere except in my life. I accept my perfect housing situation right now.

I step into this living space and know immediately this space is mine. I trust The Presence to reveal and I trust myself to listen. There is nothing other than God at work here. I live, move, and have my being in God.

When using a denial, an affirmation should always follow.

Using Scriptural References

When I am having a real hard time believing in the Allness, potency, or possibility of God, in other words, when I'm in doubt, I may choose to use scriptural references for leverage. Spiritual texts have within them immense wisdom birthed out initiated consciousness. They are also read and agreed upon by many and so the agreement energy behind them is substantial.

In the house example I gave above I mentioned the *"Lilly of the fields consciousness."* This refers to Matthew 6:28

"Consider the lilies of the field, how they grow; they toil not, neither do they spin: and yet I say unto you, even Solomon is all of his glory was not arrayed like one of these."
Matthew 6:28 and 29

Scriptural References I Frequently Use

Lilly of the field consciousness (Matthew 6:28)

"... as Jesus turned water into wine..." (John 2:1-11)

"... and Jesus says, 'you shall do even greater works than these'"... (John 14:12)

"... it is the Father which doeth the work." (John 5:19)

"From abundance I take and abundance still remains." Upanishads

Using the example of radiant health above, I may say as part of Realization:

"As Jesus turned water into wine, shifting cells within my body from unhealthy to healthy states is easy. I may not know how to do this, *but the Father within me does."*

Commitment to Affirmative Prayer Practice

A prayer stands on it own and once realized doesn't need to be repeated. It is done and known within the body. How long might this take? It depends. I have spoken a prayer to be done within minutes and never uttered it again as the shift within me took place followed by external evidence.

I have also worked a prayer treatment over months until I knew and knew that I knew. I spoke one prayer to then have another aspect of it revealed and return with a slightly different knowing. Using the example earlier of my daughter leaving home, my prayer was to Trust the Presence of God. Once this prayer was realized I then stepped into money fears around my daughter. Knowing my prayer was about me and my fear, my next set of prayers were to know the Support of God.

Dr. Ernest Holmes was known to pray for several days with one prayer before he knew and *"knew that he knew"* all was God, and This Presence was him and worked through him. He "treated" a gentleman who was a heavy alcoholic. Alcoholism at the time was not seen as a disease. There was incredible judgment in the community for this condition, and not much hope, if any of recovery. Dr. Holmes sat in prayer for two days until he had convinced his own mind and had opened to the realization that God was the Source of this man, not his alcohol. In prayer he saw beyond a condition into the Truth.

There is a word-of-mouth about Dr. Holmes in prayer for the school he administered in Los Angeles. They were $15,000 short of funds in the 1950s or 1960s, which in today's dollars is close to $200,000. He sat in prayer and affirmed and denied until he knew that he was the $15,000 he was seeking. As God is all there is, and all support, the money he desired for greater service was him. There was no separation. It is said that once he completed the prayer within a 24 hour window a former student stopped by to deliver a tithe check for $15,000.

Affirmative prayer is not wishful thinking. It is the consistent, work in shifting the unconscious patterns into the alignment with the Truth of God. It is shifting that which is unconscious into now conscious choice. It is aligning unconscious, untrained thought with Spiritual Truth. The practice is a discipline.

Now it's your turn. Continue with the prayer you started with.

Step One: God is:

Step Two: I am:

Step Three:

Therefore, I claim:

I accept:

I deny:

I know:

Notes:

CHAPTER 6
THANKSGIVING

"If the only prayer you said was 'thank you,' that would be enough." Meister Eckhart

When affirmative prayer was first used by Dr. Ernest Holmes, step four, thanksgiving was the first step of treatment. Prayer began from the state of gratitude. With the evolution of Affirmative Prayer, the order changed. There are times, however, that I begin speaking words of gratitude as a precursor to entering into Step One Recognition.

When the Realization Step is complete and felt; there is a natural desire to speak words of gratitude.

When I speak my words of Thanksgiving, I give thanks for the seed idea which has been planted into my mind, the initial stages of the rooting and the knowing that in my mind, It is Done. So, when I speak Thanksgiving, I often say so.

"I am grateful that this Affirmative Prayer is spoken, realized, and done in my mind, The Mind of God."

I may speak to the "what" that is done.

"I give thanks my body has responded to the Truth which has already been spoken and is acting the healing out right now."

"I give thanks that Jesus said, "It is done unto you, as you believe," and I believe and It is Done."

"I celebrate through the act of Thanksgiving the power of the Word spoken through

me."

You will notice that in each of these examples I am not saying "Thank you" to God. This is intentional. Since prayer is a unifying practice, I remain congruent with the language of the internal Presence. The words Thank You reflect the idea that the Presence is dual, separate than, and outside of myself.

Some of my students like to say "Thank You Inner God," or "Thank you God within." This doesn't flow for me, and yet Affirmative Prayer needs to work for the person praying, not for anyone else.

Caution: Do not be tempted to say "thank you" in this step. "Thank you" implies separation. Prayer began with God, followed by my relatedness to the One, bringing me in mind into the One field. If I use the words "thank you" it implies something separate than me and throws me out of the field created. A great phrase to use is "I give thanks for ...."

Your turn:

Step 1: : God is ...

Step 2: I am ...

Step 3: therefore ...

Step 4: I give thanks for/that ....

```
┌──────────────────────────────────────────────────────────┐
│                   Step 1: Recognition                      │
│      God is All There is. I identify one quality of God.   │
└──────────────────────────────────────────────────────────┘
```

```
┌──────────────────────────────────────────────────────────┐
│                   Step 2:  Unification                     │
│                      God is. I am.                         │
└──────────────────────────────────────────────────────────┘
```

```
┌──────────────────────────────────────────────────────────┐
│                   Step 3:  Realization                     │
│        Therefore ... I accept, I claim, I know, I realize  │
└──────────────────────────────────────────────────────────┘
```

```
┌──────────────────────────────────────────────────────────┐
│                   Step 4:  Thanksgiving                    │
│                   I give thanks that ...                   │
└──────────────────────────────────────────────────────────┘
```

Notes:

CHAPTER 7
STEP 5: RELEASE

The final step of Spiritual Mind Treatment is to release or let go of the treatment. I often say "I release this prayer into the Law," meaning I no longer hold onto the energy which has welled up within me. I let it go and I let my attachment to the words go so that the Universal Intelligence or Undifferentiated Good which is now activated within me is available to move me into fulfillment.

Science of Mind often uses the metaphor of planting a seed. The prayer is a "planting" of a deep desire into the unconscious/subjective mind and I let it go so germination may take place. Continuing to revisit the prayer, is akin to pulling the plant out of the ground repeatedly to see if the roots are growing. I disturb the process through my demonstration of faithlessness. Letting go means letting go.

The Law referred to above is the precision or operation in which the Universe works. The Universal Intelligence, God, reflects Itself through the individual and collective consciousness. I release my prayer from my new embodiment of Good I have just spoken into the Law, the precision which must manifest the internal external.

Step 5: *I release this prayer into the heart and hands of God, which reside within me.*

Step 5: *I release this prayer into the Law knowing it has been activated, set in motion.*

Step 5: *I release this prayer and call it done.*

The final words are "And So It Is" which is one interpretation of the word Amen. In essence, we are saying, "It is Done." It is our prayer punctuation.

Now, let's string all five steps together, using my example for Health.

Recognition: God is All there Is. There is not God AND anything; there is God AS everything. God is the Good that I seek. God is Health.

Unification: God is Health, also known as Wholeness. The Wholeness of God is the very fabric of Who and What I am. As God is Whole, I am Wholeness in form.

Realization: My body radiates the healthy energy of God's Good. I now recognize the health of God pulsing through each and every vein in my body. My cells scream out the health of God which they are and as they multiply, they multiple this Good. My energy reflects this health, too. I am revitalized and nourished through the Word of Good. I allow and invite this prayer to become my body, that I may feel and know God within my very body temple. I can feel it now. The Truth is my body always has been the Truth of God, the Temple of God, the place of the Most High. I realize it now. I accept it now. My sight is taken off of the visible realm and placed into and as the invisible Truth of God. My body is Whole. God's miraculous Good is operating within my being. Perfect assimilation, digestion, and release happen now. My body's set point is Health. My body's set point is God.

Thanksgiving: I give thanks my body has responded to the Truth which has already been spoken and is acting the healing out right now.

Release: I release this prayer into the Law knowing it has been activated, set in motion.

And So It Is. Amen.

Step 1: Recognition
God is All There is. I identify one quality of God.

Step 2: Unification
God is. I am.

Step 3: Realization
Therefore ... I accept, I claim, I know, I realize

Step 4: Thanksgiving
I give thanks that ...

Step 5: Release
I release this prayer into the activity of Love ...

And So It Is.
Amen.

Taking what you've built, complete your prayer below.

Problem/Desire:

Treatment Intention:

Step One, Recognition:

Step Two, Unification:

Step Three, Realization:

Step Four, Thanksgiving:

Step Five, Release:

And So It Is. Amen.

CHAPTER 8
AFTER THE PRAYER: ACTION

"Treat and move your feet." New Thought Motto

Affirmative Prayer, or Spiritual Mind Treatment activates the creative process of mind. As an idea is planted and takes hold within, then the potential to bring the prayer into form exists. This is done through intuitive action that arises from prayer.

There are several stages of spiritual development and maturation. Most people come to prayer, initially, because they want to get something. This is not a bad thing. Desire, as I mention often is "of the Father." Desire is a pulling forward out of love. When I follow love, something magical happens each time. When I pray from my head out what I think I ought to have or want, I have yet to receive it.

Affirmative Prayer is about becoming. Becoming requires action for embodiment. When I pray to get or have something and then don't listen to what is mine to do and steam roll ahead with my agenda, I've cancelled the prayer I say I've wanted.

As my spiritual life has deepened and I had a direct encounter with my Soul, my experience with Affirmative Prayer shifted. I pray for that which my Soul reveals to me. For example, I moved to Phoenix several years ago to enter into silence and solitude and reveal Me to me. Then, my entire body called me to move to the Los Angeles area. My head didn't want to do this. It still doesn't. It is inconvenient, crowded, loud, bad traffic. My self-talk is doing everything it can to have me stay in Phoenix. And yet, my body yearns. With each visit I make to Los Angeles, I want more. I meet more people I love, I connect with an active spiritual community I want to be a part of, the beach beckons me, and I return to Phoenix with the feeling I have left my beloved and I cry.

I listen to this schism between my head and my heart and I know I will be following my heart and yet my head needs a bit of catch up. I enter into Affirmative Prayer to know I will follow my Soul and in doing so everything required for this fulfillment is provided.

I still pray to become that which I desire, and yet what I understand, now, is that if I am not in touch with the desire of my Soul and I am praying from my head I can forget it. I also find myself praying simply to open, accept, embrace, love, without any form of receipt. Love for love's sake. Acceptance which leads to inner peace, or strengthens the resolve for inner peace.

Praying for Right Ministry

Let me give you an example. Approximately twenty years ago I wanted to have a ministry which wasn't in a church. I wanted to meet people, and through connection, transform lives. This was my burning and yearning desire. I did my Affirmative Prayer work for clarity and later prayed to know the Wisdom of God so I could know what was mine to do.

Within several weeks, I was sitting in my home, drinking a warm cup of tea and making a list of the things that I loved. Tea was in the top three. As I wrote it down, I knew I was to start a tea company. Intuitively, it felt right.

My next set of prayers was for a name, concept, and niche. In addition, I went to the library and researched teas and tea companies. I learned tea would be the next big drink in America. It was perfectly positioned. Just as wine had taken off and micro-brewed beers before it, tea was in its infancy and would be soaring. I loved it.

I prayed for one month for detailed clarity with one of the weeks entering into silence. Then a download came with all the information I could imagine. Company name, number of teas, strategies for sale, growth plan, all of it. I captured it in a written document, went to the bank with a proposal and was given a loan within 24 hours.

I continued to build my company this way, and live my life this way. Yearning/desire/insight followed by Affirmative Prayer then taking action based upon intuitive nudging, guidance and feedback.

One of the benefits I receive from an Affirmative Prayer practice is through speaking to myself positively, I become my own advocate. I have learned to love and trust myself through this technology.

Below are some additional examples of using Affirmative Prayer within my daily practice.

After Prayer for Friendship

I entered into solitude for a three year period. My Soul desperately wanted to give birth to itself and needed me to stop all of the doing for a while and listen. I did this. After I was guided out of this period to reintegrate into social situations I felt extremely awkward. I didn't know how to make small talk. I didn't have patience for gossip, criticism, and blame. I had left many of my friendships behind and I yearned for deep meaningful connections.

My prayer then, became for community and Soul connection. Little-by-little I noticed people seeking me out. I didn't have to have a plan or work fulfilling a strategy. My intention-prayer-intuition was potent in itself. I met other spiritual leaders, authors, and interesting people who were vitally alive.

I practiced discernment. I said 'yes' to those in whose presence I became more of me. I said 'no' to intimate relationships with people who wanted to take or thought small. It was clear they made good clients, but not friends. Clarity unfolded and revealed Itself.

I prayed, felt the response to prayer, and then I acted. Pray, felt for resonance, then aced. Pray, feel, act.

After Prayer for Financial Support

While in solitude I became frightened financially as I was spending money; it was going out, yet money wasn't coming in. Although I had sufficiency, my body would on occasion go into terror. One day, I stopped my writing, went to my prayer chair and prayed until I knew the Sufficiency of God.

Within sixty minutes, my phone rang. A man whose job it was to fulfill grants for school districts called me and asked if I would be interested in doing freelance work writing grants. I was shocked. I lived in Phoenix, knew only a handful of people, and I was in solitude. Yet, he found me.

I was stunned, to say the least. He had gotten my name and number from a woman I didn't know, but knew someone, who knew someone who thought of me. Wow. The two of us spoke, I gave him my information, and went on writing.

When a prayer is clearly answered, I stop what I am doing, write it down to remind myself of the Power of God Within and Without, and I give thanks. I want to be certain to imprint the energy of answered prayer within my mind.

After Prayer for Manifesting Right Action

The year I turned fifty I wanted to host a big birthday bash. I made a list of everything I loved and Kauai was on the top of the list. That was it. I would rent a waterfront home on the islands for a week and invite my closest ten to twelve girlfriends to join me. I felt into this idea and knew it was right.

I prayed for right location before scouting. Then I'd look, gather information and choose. I prayed for clarity regarding the right friends to invite. I wanted to be with women I loved who would get along in a house together for a week. I prayed for support to make this happen on the islands. Then I would begin making phone calls. Each step of the way I prayed and responded.

More on the Creative Process

How we create replicates the creation of God. There are four steps to the Creative Process:

1. The first step is knowing, or trusting the Allness of God and training

the mind into the Truth that This Presence or Energy is **Good**. It is beneficent and generous. It doesn't withhold and punish like the limited perception believes, it gives, gives and gives some more. In the beginning, God. This is a macrocosmic view of Creation, and it is also a personal microcosmic experience. As God created, and the consciousness of God is within me, available to me, I am able to re-create utilizing this process. This process is an ongoing process which can take years, decades, or life times. It is removing the belief from within in a separate evil which is out to harm us. Abuse survivors typically take longer to reach this knowing as it requires going beyond painful experience remembered in the body into Wholeness then further into allowing love where pain once existed.

Recognizing it can take significant time and commitment to enter into the State of Oneness, doesn't need to be a deterrent. It can feel refreshing. Creation for me, has often included tremendous healing within it. To create, means I am required to bring my full self to the party, develop or express parts of me which have been latent or unripe, and heal parts of me, or my lineage, which have remained in a wounded state. When I encounter within me, the belief in duality, I embrace it and actually become a bit giddy because I realize it is the doorway into Wholeness where I had experience separateness.

2. In the Judeo-Christian story of Creation God said "Let there be light, and there was." Since the Presence of God is all that there is and indwells me, then I declare what I desire.

Knowing this wasn't enough for me to create. Desire alone, and desire with work wasn't sufficient. Manifestation didn't stick. The key for me was to identify my desire and *be willing to give it to myself.* Was I **willing to give to myself** The Support of God? Or, was I withholding from myself as a form of punishment for being unworthy? Was I withholding from me and them blaming it on God, others, or circumstance? Was I willing to give myself a life filled with love? Or would I let my traumatized past lead me forward. Was I willing to *give to myself* peace of mind? It wasn't at times as sexy as drama.

It is one thing to be clear that I could benefit from additional health or wealth. It is another thing to *be willing to give it to myself.* If I am struggling financially and then give myself permission to have wealth, my whole world changes. I grow into more of me and am stretched into a different self concept than who I am at this moment. And, the strangest thing about the human, uninitiated mind, is it wants everything to change except itself. An aspect of the Presence of God is The Giver. The Giver or Provider is the masculine principle within. I am to consciously recognize God, become more of It and then be willing to Give from Me to me.

3. The third step in the Creative Process is **receiving**. Once I give myself permission to Be someone who has, manages, and shares wealth/health/joy/love, then I must be willing *to receive It* as the receptive, feminine principle. Within me exists the energy of Receptivity. This is where issues of unhealed worth may arise. I may be willing to imagine, I may be willing to give to myself, but will I receive it? Will I energetically reach my metaphoric hands out and receive?

One of my colleagues is an Intimacy Teacher. She said the hardest part of her work is for clients to be willing to live in a greater State of Bliss. They will only go so far until Joy, Wellbeing and Fullness make them uneasy.

Researcher Dr. Brene' Brown in a Super Soul Sunday interview with Oprah Winfrey said this same thing. She said her research showed individuals are uncomfortable with Joy. When they are in the midst of it, they tend to hedge themselves emotionally, not allowing full feeling because they are preparing for the 'let down,' or the 'other shoe to drop' thereby negating the experience of Joy. To live a conscious life means to live at choice. I can choose to experience Joy, and lots of it.

I am a big fan of the reality weight loss shows on television as I enjoy watching someone allow their inner self to emerge through a challenge they have given themselves. Each show the trainer will make some comment like "the physical workout part is easy, it is facing the emotional weight which is where the work is." And, they are right. The real work comes in being willing to give oneself the body they desire and then being willing to receive it.

This past week one of the show's contestants was adopted into a family that adored and loved her. She said repeatedly, "I have not been able to accept the idea I am loveable because I was given away." She was aware her adoptive family loved her. They treated her very well. It wasn't until she was in her twenties; decades after she was adopted, she was able to receive the love she knew was right in front of her.

4. As I become what I've been willing to *give to myself* and *receive from myself*, I then **bring this as me into the world**. I actually share along the way of learning to give and to receive, yet, the world needs me Whole and in Possibility. So, God gives to me Life, I receive life and then I give aspects of God to myself and I receive the aspect given to me. Once received, I

then give to the world the I am I have become. This is the creation process.

The Truth is, all of God's nature is already given to me and present within me. The creation process is like a re-creation process or an unveiling process where I consciously engage in activating the Presence.

God is Health. As I am actively committed to being the Presence of Health as me; I give the Health to myself which already exists beneath all of my false beliefs and misunderstandings. Then I receive this from myself and behave out of this knowing. God is Health. I demonstrate health. I bring health into the world as an individual not dependent upon the health care system, teaching others how I became healthy, and making choices financially which reflect my new values.

God is Peace. As I give myself permission to be peaceful and I receive the Peace I already am, then I live my life from different behavior. The entertainment I participate in is different. How I do community changes and I choose to create with others from peace. How I organize my home and how I use electronics is different. My spending habits and conversation differs. All of this changes my world with a ripple affect into the shared world.

God is Wealth. As I give myself permission to give the wealth of God to myself, I am choosing to be a person of sufficiency and abundance. I am willing to utilize what I have financially, emotionally, and creatively for exponential growth. As I receive this desire within myself, I too behave differently. I become aware of my resources. I look at my values. I determine what is and isn't mine. I care about my time. Efficiency couples with creativity. This changes me which changes who I am in the world.

I enjoy tithing for this reason. Tithing, or giving ten percent to where I'm spiritually fed, requires me to give, receive, become and share.

God is Wisdom. As I give myself permission to accept the Wisdom that is innate within me, I realize Wisdom is the marriage between Intelligence and Love. It is the sharing of the head and heart when approaching and creating situations. As I give myself the Wisdom I already am, and I actively receive it, then I act wise. This is conscious thinking. My world changes form it. The world changes from it.

Notes:

CHAPTER 9
PRAYING FOR OTHERS

Affirmative prayer can be used to pray for others when they have requested it, and only when they have requested it. This rule is iron clad when we begin as learners of this process. Then, as we deepen in our spiritual journey and realize there is only One of us here, then we understand the prayer for another is a prayer for ourselves and the whole prayer dynamic changes.

Why is it important to ask another if we can pray for them? Because we are training ourselves to have boundaries, mind our own business, tend to our own inner world and remove our energy from the life of others that all of us may have a more potent energy field of our own.

I am aware this isn't easy. I watch students and clients want prayer for people other than themselves. Often this points to the underlying belief that if someone or something was different, I would be okay. "If my spouse had a job, I'd be okay. Therefore, I will pray for my spouse to have a job." The real prayer request here is to pray to be okay regardless of circumstances and to pray to know the Wealth of God as you. Each one of us grows into more of ourselves when we meet aspects of life we don't want. To grow into becoming more Trusting of God, may be the underlying Soul desire.

Another example of this is parents praying for their children to stop addiction. When the attention is on the addiction, then the self and the child are over looked. The key is, if you don't have permission, to go within yourself to discover where YOU require prayer. It can be learning to say 'no' or cleaning yourself up to be a good example. It could be developing strength of Spirit, Trust, or the ability to love more deeply.

However, if your child, spouse, friend, prayer partner, or client requests prayer, then the Affirmative Prayer process is spoken or written just as if the prayer was for you. It is in the first person, singular. You, as the one praying, are doing the work for yourself, as there is only One of us here. You are praying from the One Life aligning your mind with the God Mind, your heart with the One Heart and speaking the prayer on their behalf.

Since God is all there is, then speaking the prayer from The One, is spoken within your own mind as the Mind of God. You are having the realization within your own consciousness accessing The Only Consciousness which is.

Two of the Treatment steps are modified to include the person you are praying for. In Unification, you will say … *"God is, I am, and so too is (insert name here). "*

or, *"as this is True of me, this also must be True of (insert name here)."*

When praying for another, use their name or the third person singular pronouns; he, she, his, hers. A person's name is powerful and contains its own energy field. Name means Nature. Avoid using "you" as a prayer is a treatment, not a conversation.

In Realization, likewise, the name of the person will be inserted after you know the Universal Truth for yourself.

"As I radiate the Health of God, so too does (insert name here)."

"As I speak this word of Truth for myself, I also speak it for (insert name here) as (insert name here) is also the Presence of God in form."

I have discovered that as I pray to know the Presence of God in a specific way for my clients, then I am praying for me to become more of that. When I pray for Wealth or Health, I step into that field and see more of it in my life. When I pray for a deeper relationship on behalf of another, mine become richer.

Prayer for Successful House Transaction for Client Sally

Recognition: There is One Presence, One Power, and One Life Force known by many names, which I choose to call God. This Presence lives, moves, and has Its Being through all humankind giving of Itself day in and day out, without end. It is Its Nature to give, give, and give some more. Another name for God is the Giver of the Universe. All Life comes from It, All Good begins within It. And this Good is the Multiplying Presence of God.

Unification: As God is Good, as God multiplies Its Good, then this too is True of me and True of Sally. The Good of God is the Operating force within her. It can't help Itself. God Is. I am. Sally is.

Realization: And as God gives, and is giving forth right now, I claim the successful house transaction is complete right here and right now in the Mind of God and in the human dimensional form. The paperwork is completed easily and with Divine Support. The processing is flawless as the electricity of the Good is experienced with each touch of the paper and between each person involved in this transaction. This is not solely a real estate transaction this is a Love transaction. The Presence of Love is exposed as the transaction showing Itself to each person involved. The seller delights in making accommodations and both realtors work together for the highest of Sally, her realtor, the sellers, and their realtor. Record timing is underway. I know Joy all over and through the transaction.

I let go of any previously held prejudices about home transactions. I release any lies I've told myself about inefficiencies. I know right now that God is a God of Possibility, not precedence. Past records hold no energy within this transaction. This transaction is Divinely Anointed. The Power of God resides within me and I call it So. The Good within God resides with me and I call it So. And as this is True of me, it is True of Sally. Good is the order of the day. Good is the field in which I am playing. Good makes the way straight. Good is the dominant and only vibration. I know this to be True. I know this is the Only Truth as an outpouring from the Only God.

Thanksgiving: I give thanks the Present of God is at work here and always and the Power within me has spoken and it is fulfilled.

Release: I release this prayer. **And So It Is. Amen.**

Reverend Bonnie

Notes:

CHAPTER 10
QUESTIONS ON AFFIRMATIVE PRAYER

Question #1: How do I know what is and what isn't a Quality of God?

Answer #1: *Emma Curtis Hopkins said in her work Scientific Mental Christian Practice, that Good is another name for God. Meaning, that which we agree upon as Good which existed before I was born and will remain after I die, Eternal Good, is another name for God.*

There are some commonly accepted qualities such as Love, Peace, Joy, Good, True Abundance, Wealth, Creativity, Prosperity, Light, Health, Self Expression, Substance, Intelligence, and Perfection.

There are secondary qualities of God which exists; such as Compassion, which is born out of Love, and Restoration which born out of Substance. Like primary and secondary colors, new is made through the melding of secondary qualities. For example, Wisdom is made of Love and Intelligence. I want to guide you into using the primary qualities, and yet what I know, is affirming your Highest Idea of God is enough. And, when students have affirmed Enoughness and worked with it, they grow themselves into a consciousness willing to accept Abundance. Therefore, don't get hung up on qualities. You may use the above list, or make up your own. The key is to link what you believe to be Eternally Good, True and without harm.

Question #2: I do my affirmative prayer work and feel great. Later in the day I may meet a circumstance that is contrary to the prayer and then feel defeated. How do I deal with this? An example of this is my rent is due in two weeks, I had a roommate who signed the lease and moved out and now I am stuck with more apartment than money. I immediately go in my mind to what I'm going to lose. I feel like I need to sell my car, give up on my new CD and career I'm wanting to launch, or lose my apartment. I see no win.

Answer #2: *The solution to every problem is more God. It is accessing more of the internal Good within and living from this place. Changing one's consciousness; changing one's mind is the hardest work we will ever do; and also the most rewarding. To go from the first response thought of "I won't have enough; I must therefore lose" to the belief and trust in Sufficiency as a birthright of Consciousness is a big mental shift. Making this mental shift means you could succeed!! And a person who succeeds and has a good life is a very different person than one who doesn't and blames circumstances around her.*

Although it is hard to admit to ourselves, we may not like to live on the edge of survival; yet if it is what we know, then it is comfortable to us. Moving outside of a comfort zone is uncomfortable by definition. It is this raw, vulnerable space where we experience the most mind chatter. Let this deflated feeling be an indication to you that you are in the courageous zone. You could be the artist with a thriving CD and a ministry which affords you the opportunities you can only dream of now. And, this requires accountability, leaving excuses behind, action aligned with your vision and a willingness to be your own best support team. The journey is worth it.

You may be required to take the actions you mentioned and you may not. You are developing the consciousness of self love and support. This means, regardless of circumstance, you decide you are worth supporting and taking a stand for.

Speaking a prayer is one thing. Dwelling in the energy of a prayer is another. And living out of it; yet another. Scripture says to pray without ceasing. This means to me the recognition that I live, move, and have my being in God regardless of circumstances. And, as I continue to practice calling forth more God in the midst.

In your shoes, I would practice embodying more Trust and Courage taking guided action. If you desire a new room mate, then tell your friends, post it at your church, let people at work know, tell your community, pray and practice discernment in your choice. God really is Good and It can be trusted.

Question #3: How do I know that my prayer works?

Answer #3: *Metaphysicians often speak of affirmative prayer using a garden analogy. It is said that the seed is the like a request, planted into the soil, which represents the unconscious mind, and nurtured, sunned, and watered by the Love of God. When we become anxious and want a result quicker than its natural unfoldment, it would be like a gardener, unable to see the plant's roots, pulling it out of the ground for examination. Patience, prayer, and action are a part of the creation/manifestation process. When a prayer is complete, you will know for you will have changed and/or the result will be made visible.*

If your prayer isn't being answered through or by you, then in your quiet daily communion, inquire what else is yearning to come through you and follow that. For example, you may pray to know God as Wealth and you want to take guitar lessons but you feel as though you can't afford it. Find a way to give yourself the lessons. That may open the floodgate to your wealth.

Question #4: Does Affirmative Prayer get easier the more I do it? I have been doing it now for two weeks and it feels awkward and weird. Will this change?

Answer #4: *Yes, affirmative prayer becomes easier the more you practice it. The key is to use your own words that lift you up. You are training your thoughts to align with the Good of God. I believe I felt awkward and like I was faking it for at least a year, maybe longer. I received spotty results, and yet when I look backward today, I realize the immense amount of healing/revealing which took place in my early studies. Most new students see and feel results immediately. It took me longer. Give yourself patience and compassion. This work is powerful, you are powerful.*

Question #5: If God knows my heart, why do I have to pray?

Answer #5: *You pray so that you may know the Presence of God within you and you may know your own heart. Implied within your question is the idea of an external God who takes care of you. As you open to the Presence of God which is the very fullness of your being, the desire to pray and deepen grows.*

Question: #6: Is Affirmative Prayer the only style of prayer you use?

Answer #6: *No. I use the Show Me Prayer when I am lost, in overwhelm and don't remember. This prayer, my mentor, calls the Las Vegas prayer. Show me, Inner Wisdom, so clearly that it resonates brightly like a lit up sign in Las Vegas.*

I also use the Life Visioning process as taught by Rev. Dr. Michael Beckwith and available on CDs and book. This process prepares me for listening deeply to my Soul. It is often a precursor to Affirmative Prayer. I meditate often in silence and I love to contemplate on a spiritual idea, concept, or scripture. And, none of this matters if I don't act out of what I know to be my Soul, or Inner Presence of Good.

Question #7: When do you pray? Do you have a set prayer schedule or do it when you need it?

Answer#7: *I hope to become the living embodiment of prayer; praying without ceasing. And in Truth, I am, and each of us are. We are walking signals of desire,* *worth, vision, and who we see ourselves to be. However, I believe your question is more about the practice of this technology. I have a three hour spiritual practice process each morning. This allows me to show up clean for the clients I serve. I do a meditative walk. I journal. I sit in silent meditation. I contemplate and then I enter into prayer. I do my own prayer and pray for my clients; going deeper into each intention.*

Question #8: How would you describe God and prayer?

Answer #8: *God is Pure Undifferentiated Divine Love. It is All there Is. It Gives forth. Prayer is communion with this Inner Presence. I used to pray to and believe in a God outside of me, exclusively. Then I practiced Affirmative Prayer for decades at which point I knew the Presence was an Inner Presence. Just as the realization took hold I then tapped into the External All Presence. The Outer/Inner/All Presence of Love. I gained this insight through meditation, visioning, practicing my insights and Affirmative Prayer.*

CHAPTER 11

WORKING WITH A PRAYER PRACTITIONER

Affirmative Prayer practitioners exists in Science of Mind Centers and many New Thought Spiritual Centers. A prayer practitioner has studied the science and application of this technology for at least four years, passed a written and oral test and kept current through continuing education and active practice. This is a profession with professional standards and conduct.

Each practitioner sets their own price. Some provide a prayer only and others provide spiritual counseling services along with the prayer. The counseling sessions consist of teaching the client how to think in order to align their thinking with Spirit until Spirit is the predominate thought within them. These sessions are confidential. They begin and end in prayer. This is how I practice.

As with any other professional, research and trusting your gut is helpful. Some of the practitioners specialize. They may teach the Universal Principles in one or two specialty areas such as relationships, courage, wholeness, health, success or money. Use your discretion when choosing a practitioner, as you would any other professional.

I have worked with a practitioner every other week faithfully since 1993, almost twenty years. I cannot imagine my life without a professional dedicated to my spiritual growth and development. If you desire deeper communion, quicker manifestations, and someone praying for your highest good, try a practitioner for two months and track in your journal the difference you notice. If your practitioner isn't a fit, don't hesitate to change until you find one that is. A prayer practitioner is a very personal decision. Sessions are confidential and sharing can become deep.

In addition to providing private sessions, prayer practitioners teach and offer additional services. I have attended several mediated gatherings between neighbors as a "friend" while being silently in prayer throughout negotiations. I have been in undercover prayer in business meetings as an "observer" or "consultant" and I have made hospital visits praying during surgeries or during a recovery period. I have done house blessings and conducted various spiritual rituals for individuals, couples, and families.

What Is a Practitioner Paid For?

A practitioner is paid, like any professional, for their time and talent. In this case, talent is the cultivated, developed consciousness that is brought into prayer.

Some things I look for in a practitioner:

- Do they walk their talk? This is evidenced by how they speak and behave in situations outside of a session.
- Can they provide me with references I can call prior to meeting with them?
- Do they do their work in person? Over the phone? Or a combination?
- Do they have an active spiritual practice? Ask them. I want someone committed more than I am to practice as my advisor.
- What is their style? Are they hard, clear, accountable, and direct? Do they have a need for me to change in some way? Are they compassionate, accepting and receptive? A combination of these styles?
- What do they charge?
- Do they pray for me throughout the week?

Where To Find Prayer Practitioners

Centers for Spiritual Living

www.csl.org

Here you can place a prayer request online, or you can locate a center in your area. Each center has a team of prayer practitioners.

Affiliated New Thought Centers

www.emersoninstitute.edu

This site lists centers, may of which have prayer practitioners.

Agape International Center of Truth

www.agapelive.com

Agape has a prayer line to call with request and a list of available prayer practitioners.

Notes:

CHAPTER 12
SAMPLE PRAYERS

Prayer for Perfect Health

Perceived Problem: Low energy, minimal get-up-and-go.

Treatment: Perfect Health

Recognition: God is all there is. There is nothing other than God. God is Perfect Divine Health. There is not God as Health and sickness, there is Only and Always God the Good. God is It. The Alpha and the Omega, the beginning and the end and everything in between God is the Unmanifest and the manifest.

Unification: As God is Health and I am one with this Presence made of God-stuff, I too am health. I am the emanation of Good in the form of health.

Realization: My body radiates the healthy energy of God's Good. I now recognize the health of God pulsing through each and every vein in my body. My cells scream out the health of God which they are and as they multiply, they multiple this Good. My energy reflects this health, too. I am revitalized and nourished through the Word of Good. I allow and invite this prayer to become my body, that I may feel and know God within my very body temple. I can feel it now. I am the vitality of God. My health has turned the corner. God's miraculous Good is operating within my being. Perfect assimilation, digestion, and release happens. My body's set point is Health. My body's set point is God. I feel Good. I feel God.

Thanksgiving: I give thanks for the every present generosity of God's Health, always available and ample now working through me, as me.

Release: I release this prayer into the Law of God which operates as Divine Love. Life is Good. **And So It Is.**

Note: As prayer is Truth felt in the body, as mentioned in Chapter Eight, action follows. Praying for perfect health may or may not require a shift in action. A dear friend of mine prayed for right weight. She was guided, then, to tell herself every morning and when she passed the mirror how deeply she loved her. Without changing her diet or exercise, she dropped thirty pounds from her body in one month.

Then, she was guided into exercise. She wanted it. It fascinated her, caught her attention, moved her. She converted a room in her home into a gym and found herself gravitating toward it and working out regularly. Not because her head told her she should or she needed to prove something, but because of a deep inner desire.

When I prayed for perfect health I was guided to a medical intuitive who suggested I have my thyroid checked with my doctor, and I did. Prayer is an interactive and inner-active practice.

I tend to listen to the prayer that is rising within my Soul and pray for that.

Prayer to Soften Anger and Rage

Perceived Problem: I tend to fly off the handle in rage, quick to anger around everyone, especially those I love.

Treatment: To know the Peace of God.

Recognition: God is all there is. There is not God *and* me, there is God *as* me. God, the One. God, the Only. God the Good I am seeking, God, Peace.

Unification: As God is All There Is, and It Is Peace, then I am an expression of this Eternal Beingness, I am the Peace of God in form, I am Peace Itself. I am peaceful.

Realization: I realize the Peace of God through and as my Being Nature. I am the presence of Peace. I honor the energy that pulses throughout my body system. I release pent up energy in ways that serve my body, my integrity, and with honor of those around me. I realize I hold the inner control panel of my responses; I am always at choice and I wake up to this choice now.

I embody the I AM Consciousness of God, which at Its core is the Presence of Peace. Not passive, good for nothing, without energy inert. The Peace of God that changes everything through Its conscious activity as Me. The Peace that makes the difference by me being the difference. I say *no* when I need to say *no* and *yes* when a *yes* is in order. I am congruent, clean, and powerful in my discernment.

I refuse to hurt myself or another. I allow the Grace of God to teach me, guide me, move me and inform into my next right action. If I'm to work with a master in this area, I do. If I'm to read or study, I accept. I am open and willing to be, do, and have the Peace of God as me.

I naturally gravitate toward people, places, and situations that reinforce the Peace I am. I sit in silence. I take walks. I change what I eat and drink, in honor of who I am and who I am becoming. All of me aligns with the Peace of God, as God.

I release my belief in heredity as power. I release my belief in Power as aggression and open to the Truth that the Greater power is Peace. God is. I am.

Thanksgiving: I give thanks it is done.

Release: I release this prayer along with any old residue belief into the transforming power of God. **And So It Is.**

Prayer for Self Confidence

Perceived Issue: I don't like myself. I can't trust myself. I am stupid and I make bad decisions.

Treatment: To know I am loving and lovable. To trust myself.

Recognition: God is all there is. God is. There is nothing other than, in addition to, separate from the Presence and Power of God.

Unification: I am a manifest form of God the Good. I am the Presence of God in form with all of the gifts, promises, and possibilities available in me as within The One.

Realization: Realizing I am One with and as God; I allow myself to feel into the Love of God. I awaken to this vibration; this Truth and I realize I am this vibration and Truth. God is Love. I am loved. I practice this within myself. I speak words of Love to me. I give myself compassion and grace. I open to the energy of the Love of God.

I deny any appearance or experience that I've trained myself to believe in as real. The past is over and done, today I live in the energy of today. I allow my feelings to arise and I honor and love them. I choose my actions from a conscious place of the Present love of God.

I deny the idea of being stupid. I am the intelligence of God. I deny the idea that I don't know how to decide, I make decisions all day long. From this moment forward I see myself as my Inner God; The Holy Spirit of Good sees me; as Whole. I let go of the lies I've been told in my life that I won't amount to anything. This is a lie. Nothing amounts more than me or less than me as I am God Itself. And, that is enough. I accept the Love as God as me, and I live from the Love of God as me.

Thanksgiving: I give thanks for the opportunity to create and recreate in my life. I give thanks for the opportunity to change my mental patterning. And, I give thanks that the Love of God guiding me.

Release: I release this prayer into the Law of fulfillment and allow it to be. **And So It Is. Amen.**

Prayer for Right Work

Perceived Issue: I was let go from my job; it is no longer needed in today's economy. I would like to change professions using my skills of serving customers, and growing markets. I do not know where to start or what's available.

Treatment: To find the right work for me right now and reduce the fear I'm experiencing.

Recognition: There is One God, One Life, One Presence in operation right now and always. It operates through and as all life, including mine; it is Life Itself. This Life Presence is the Divine Orchestrator behind and within all Good and right action.

Unification: I align with this Good of God right now, as I am the Good of God embodied in physical form. The operating faculty of the Universe pumps through my blood. It is the very Isness of who I am. I am the Good that I seek. I am It.

Realization: As God is all there Is, It is Good, and I express this Goodness, I claim for myself right here and right now the fulfillment of right work. I willingly and generously bring forth my gifts, talents and love for my own self joy of self expression and wealth and for the overflowing benefit of humankind. I serve, and I am served. I give forth and the overflowing givingness of God is activated and bringing forth my Good beyond measure. Good to good; God to god.

I know there is a right fit for me and as this is so, it is wanting me and searching for me actively, as well. I know I find right work and right work finds me. I sit right now in the energy of serving customers and growing markets and as I dwell here in the state of It is Done. I feel the energy of creation, love, and service. I feel the Support of God as my support. There is One of us here and it is realized in right work, right now.

Thanksgiving: I give thanks for my satisfying job and its fulfillment.

Release: I release this prayer with the conviction it is done. **And So It is.**

Prayer for Wealth

Perceived Issue: I seem to always be short on money. I can predict it. I feel it. I expect it, and I can't seem to shift it. I want to know the Wealth of God in all aspects of my life; especially money.

Treatment: To know the Support of God as financial wealth.

Recognition: I know God is All there is and from where all things flow. I know God as the Giver of Good to Itself in, through, and as all situations and the Receiver from Itself. It enacts perfect circulation.

Unification: And this perfect circulation happens within me. As there is Only One; then, by definition, It is me and I am in It. God is; I am. God gives through Its creation and receives as Its creation. I enact the giving and receiving nature of God and Its Good in all forms.

Realization: Today I turn my attention away from the belief in scarcity. I release the lie of not-enoughness as when I speak of not-enough, I am speaking of the Presence of God as limited, and this is a bold face lie. I sit in and with this prayer as the feeling tone of enoughness ripens through, within and as me as it reaches the Truth of Sufficiency and then overflows from Abundance.

I feel the fulfillment of God and I act from It. Today I give financially as a symbol of the support of God. I give money to the electric company and I receive the electricity I desire. I give to the grocery store and I receive food from the store. I give to where I am spiritually fed and I receive the food of Truth. I enact the Givingness of God and I receive from the act of giving. Give; receive; give; receive. And all of this is of and from God and with gratitude. Today I am awake to the giving I do and to the receiving I have. And, I invite in more.

I release the belief that I am victimized in any way by finances. I am powerful. The Power of God pumps through my veins and I use my discerning wisdom and stewardship abilities with my finances. Instead of shutting down out of fear, I practice opening to possibilities. I am honest with myself in relationship to money and how I behave in relationship to it. Money is a form of energy. Money represents self lovingness in physical form. Money supports me although it is only one tangible form of support. It is not *my* Support. God is my Support from which ideas and money flow.

Jesus said "it is done unto you, as you believe." Today I evoke the belief in the Consciousness of Plenty. I see plenty in all forms today and as I see it reminds me of the Truth; God is All there Is; It is Good; and It is Plentiful.

Thanksgiving: I am grateful for the Plenty of God and Its givingness to and through me.

Release: I release this prayer knowing It is fulfilled. **And So It Is. Amen.**

Prayer for Intimate Partnership

Perceived Issue: I want to share my love with someone special and I just can't seem to find him.

Treatment: I receive the partnership I desire.

Recognition: There is One Life and that is the Life of God.

Unification: And, that One Life is my life now. There is no separation between The One Presence and me. It lives, moves, and has Its beingness in, through, and as me, expressing Itself with permission and invitation as the very Life Force that Is.

Realization: And I give my permission to the Holy God within me to demonstrate through me as Divine Love. To lead me, guide me, fulfill me as if I am in partnership right here and right now.

The qualities of God I look for in another; compassion, adoration, support, creativity, joy, contribution, I now give to myself and express as myself right now. I become the partner within me that I have desired without. I become the Love I wish to receive and I give that love liberally. I practice Grace, Forgiveness, and Inclusion right now as my way of living. I give thanks for my life today, single and happy as I make space within my life for my partner. I prepare in conscious and receive my desires as me as I clear space and honor the embodiment as the other making their way to me now.

I remain open, available, and willing. I try new things. I go new places, and I remind myself the Truth, *in God all things are possible*. I let go of the lies I tell myself about my unworthiness. I let go of the notion I am too … anything to be with my beloved. It is a lie that I am too thin, too educated, too young, too hurt. I release any belief in hurt right here and now as my set point. The past is over. Today is new, and I live, move, and have my being in love.

I know as I pray to receive my beloved, he is calling me forward consciously or unconsciously, as well. The call is strong and the finding is easy. I know when I meet him that It is Done.

Thanksgiving: I give thanks for feeling my beloved within me now. I give thanks that the Truth sets me Free. I celebrate the generosity of Spirit.

Release: And I release this prayer into the Law, knowing it was fulfilled before I spoke it. **And So It Is. Amen**.

Prayer to Forgive

Perceived Issue: I have made my dear friend, June, wrong for a recent choice she made. I can't seem to be loving and I want to be.

Treatment: My prayer is to forgive or let go of the funk I am holding attached to June. I want to know and see her, again, as love.

Recognition: There is One Life and That is the Life of God. Divine Love, without Condition, God.

Unification: And as there is Only One, Outpicturing as many, I recognize that the I am Consciousness of Love resides within me. I am the Love of God made flesh.

Realization: As God is all there is, and there is only One of us here, then I claim right now, as the Love of God I am, I release, drop, and let go of the judgment I hold against June. I experience the dropping, and letting go within my own consciousness of judgment toward June AND toward myself. I have made her wrong for her decision. So I release myself from any decision I have made that I have perceived to be either right or wrong. Better or worse. Greater than or less than. A decision is in alignment with the Good of God or not. It doesn't hold a value. I Trust the Presence of God as me and I Trust the Presence of God as June and so I release the non-sense that I know what is best for June or any other.

I retrieve the energy back into my core as The One Energy, God. God is Love. I give forth (for-give) Love. God is Grace. I give forth Grace. As I give forth this Grace I recognize I am giving forth from Me and to me. God is all there is and It is Good.

Thanksgiving: I give thanks for the Love of God I am.

Release: I release this prayer celebrating Love. Love is. **And so It Is. Amen.**

ABOUT THE AUTHOR

Rev. Dr. Bonnie Barnard knew at age five she was to grow up and become a minister, serving God by serving humanity. As a girl born in the 1960s, this was an interesting proposition as there were no women ministers in any of the churches she'd attended and her Episcopal Church referred to ministers as "Father." She thought "Father Bonnie" sounded odd, and yet it didn't quell her little girl desire.

Her undergraduate degree is in Religious Studies from the University of Puget Sound, Tacoma, WA. She became a Religious Science Practitioner, utilizing Affirmative Prayer and teaching Spiritual Principle in the late 1990s. She studied this through Holmes Institute, Seattle Campus. She went on to ministerial training through Holmes Institute to complete through Vici Derrick Ministries and later Emerson Theological Institute where she received her Doctorate in Divinity.

Rev. Dr. Bonnie wrote a book on forgiveness entitled Forgive Your Way to Freedom in 2004 and traveled the United States and Canada teaching forgiveness practices. In 2009, 2010, and 2011, she entered into contemplative solitude where she "birthed her Soul." She wrote two books, published in 2013, A Year of Go(o)d: Daily Lessons for the Mystic in Training and Affirmative Prayer: Becoming Your Own Answered Prayer.

www.bonniebarnard.com

Made in the USA
Columbia, SC
26 October 2020

23529483R00055